THE PICTURE BOOK OF

HORSES

Copyright © 2024 Clara Fern

All rights reserved.

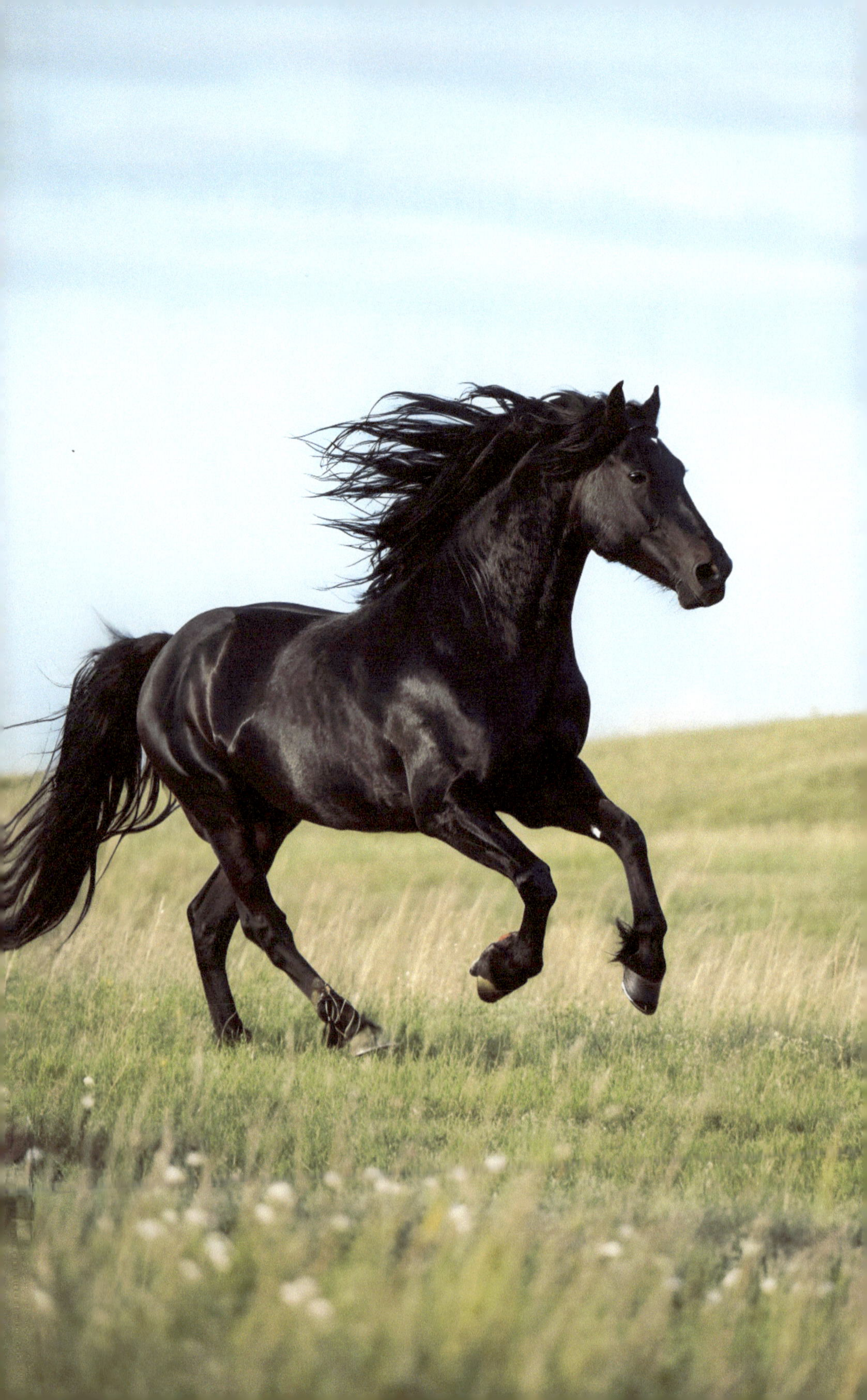

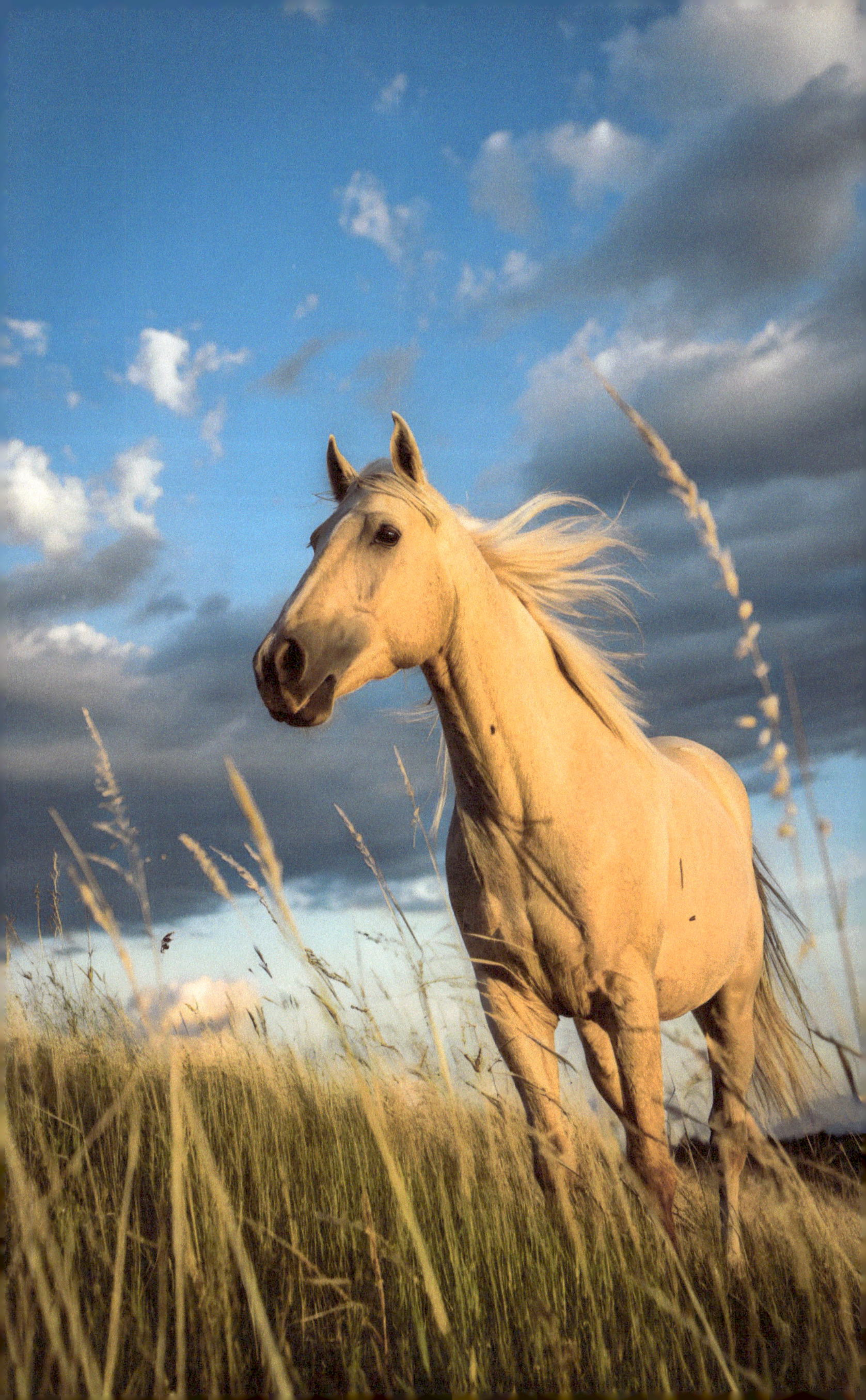

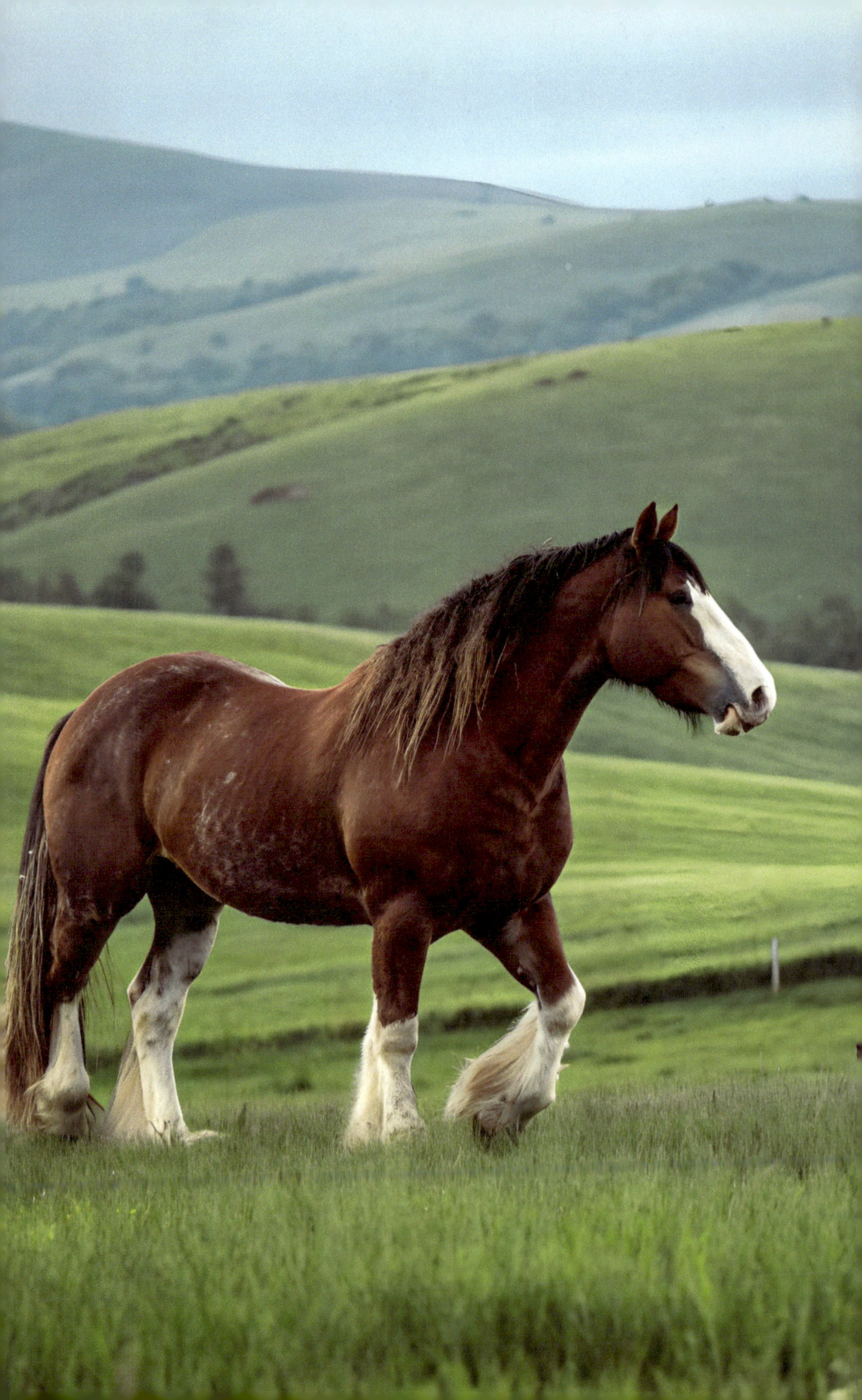

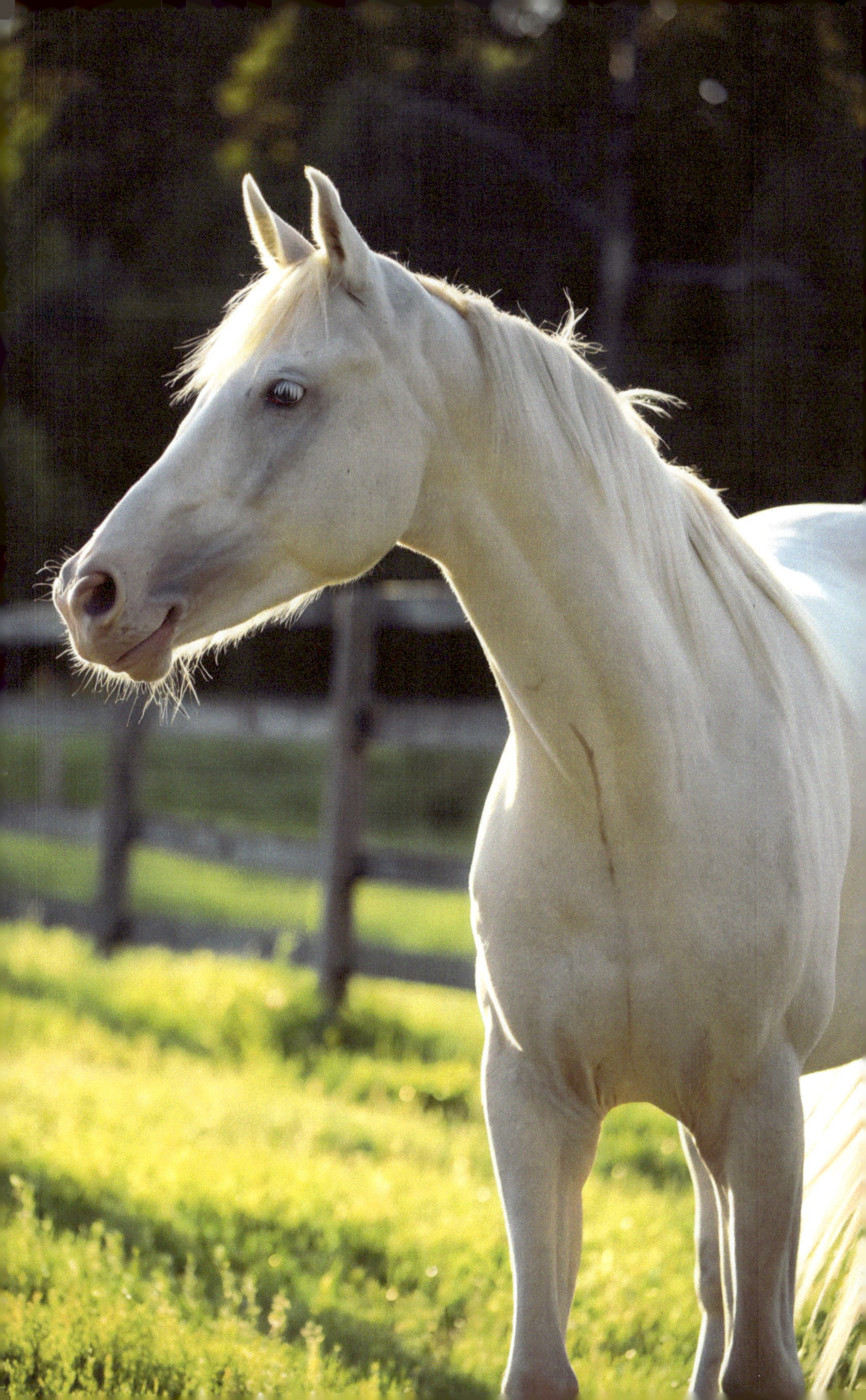

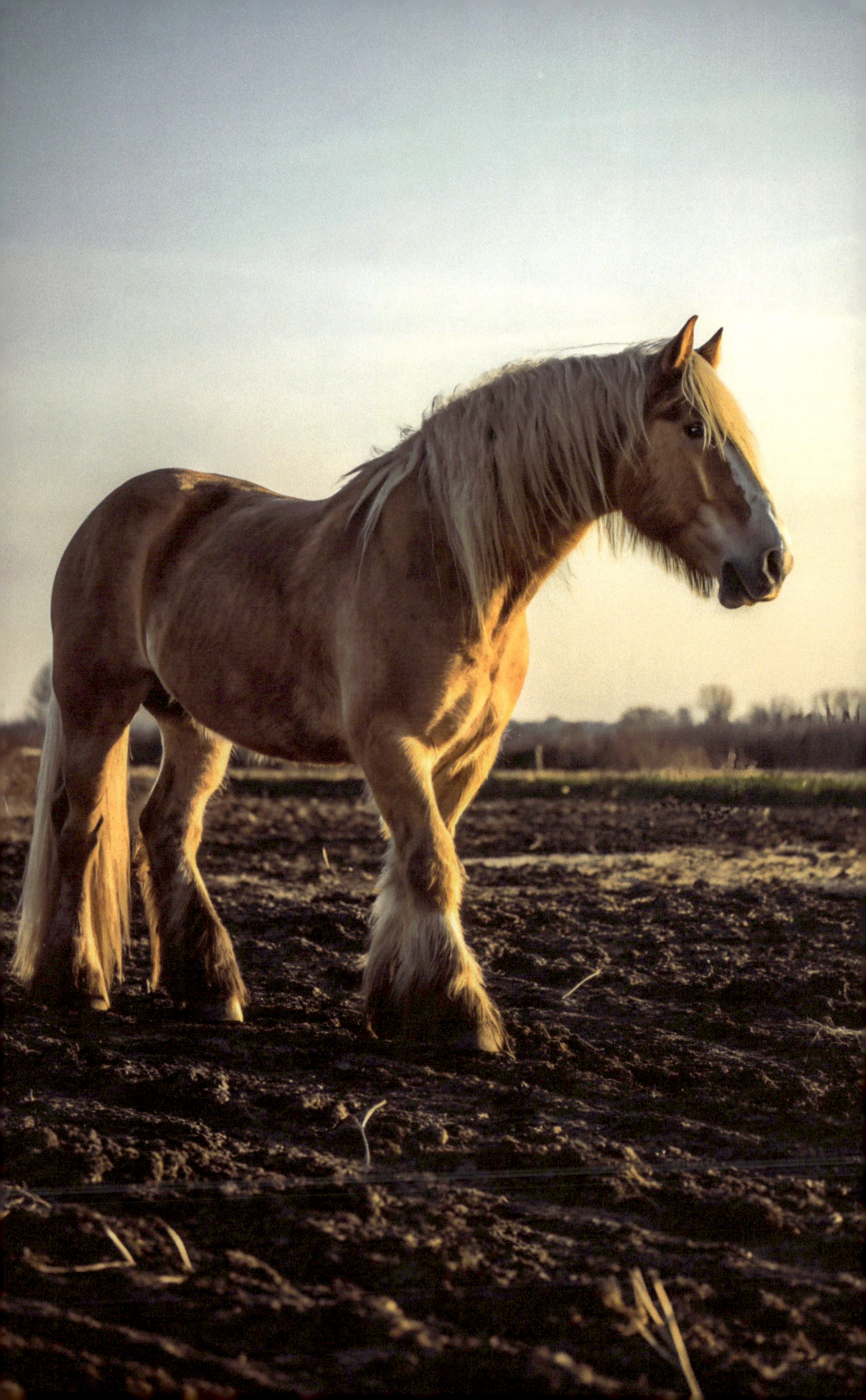

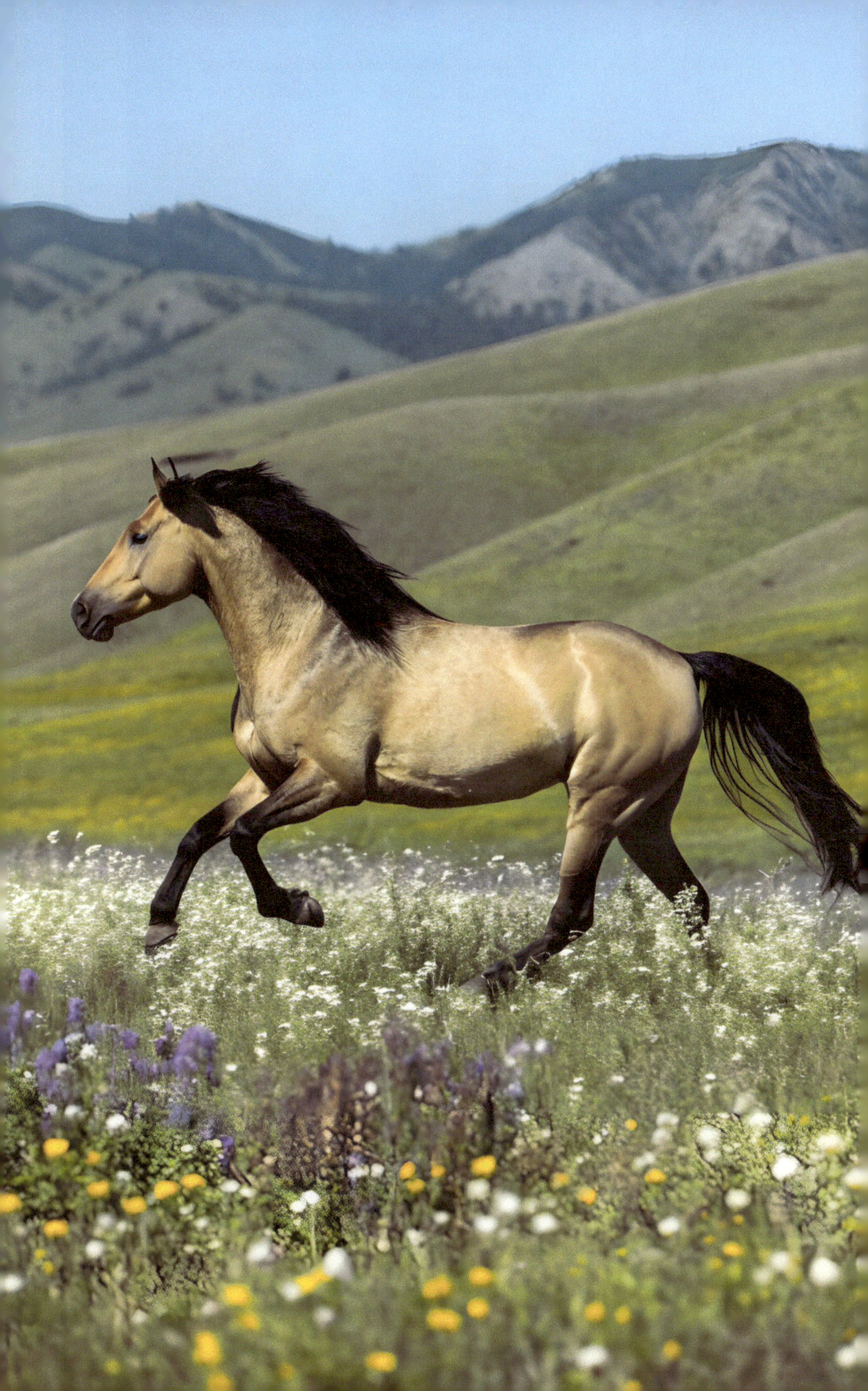

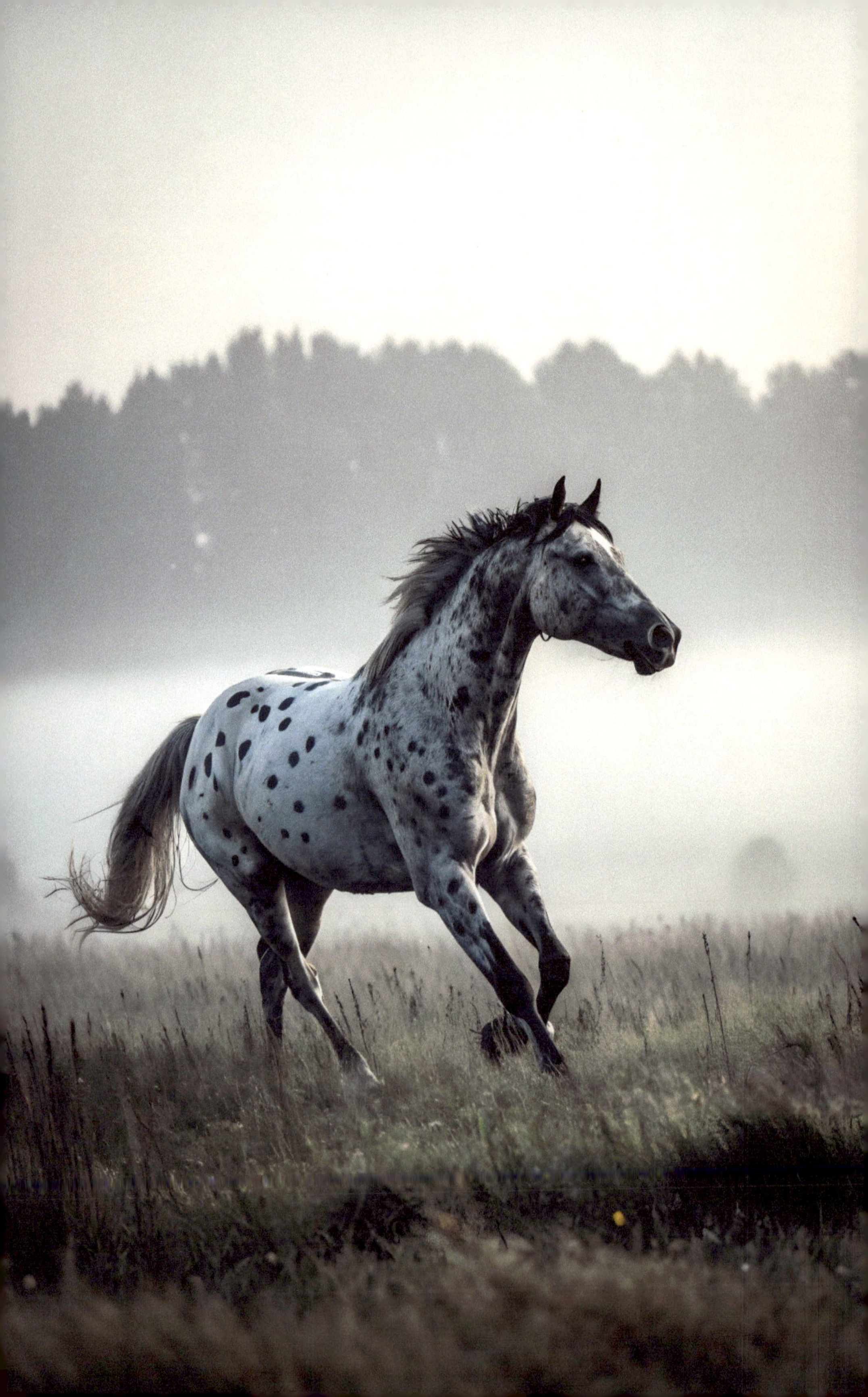

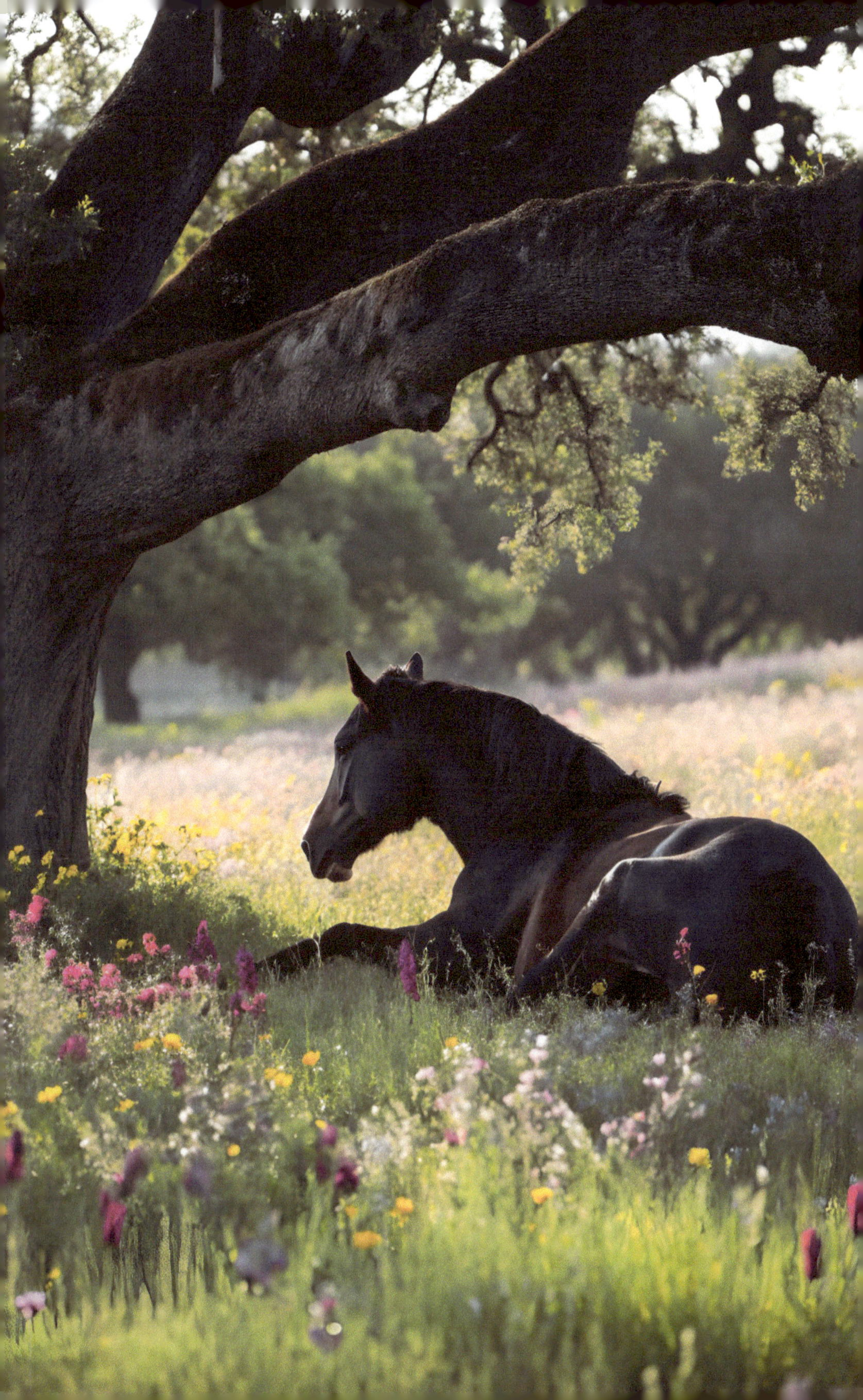

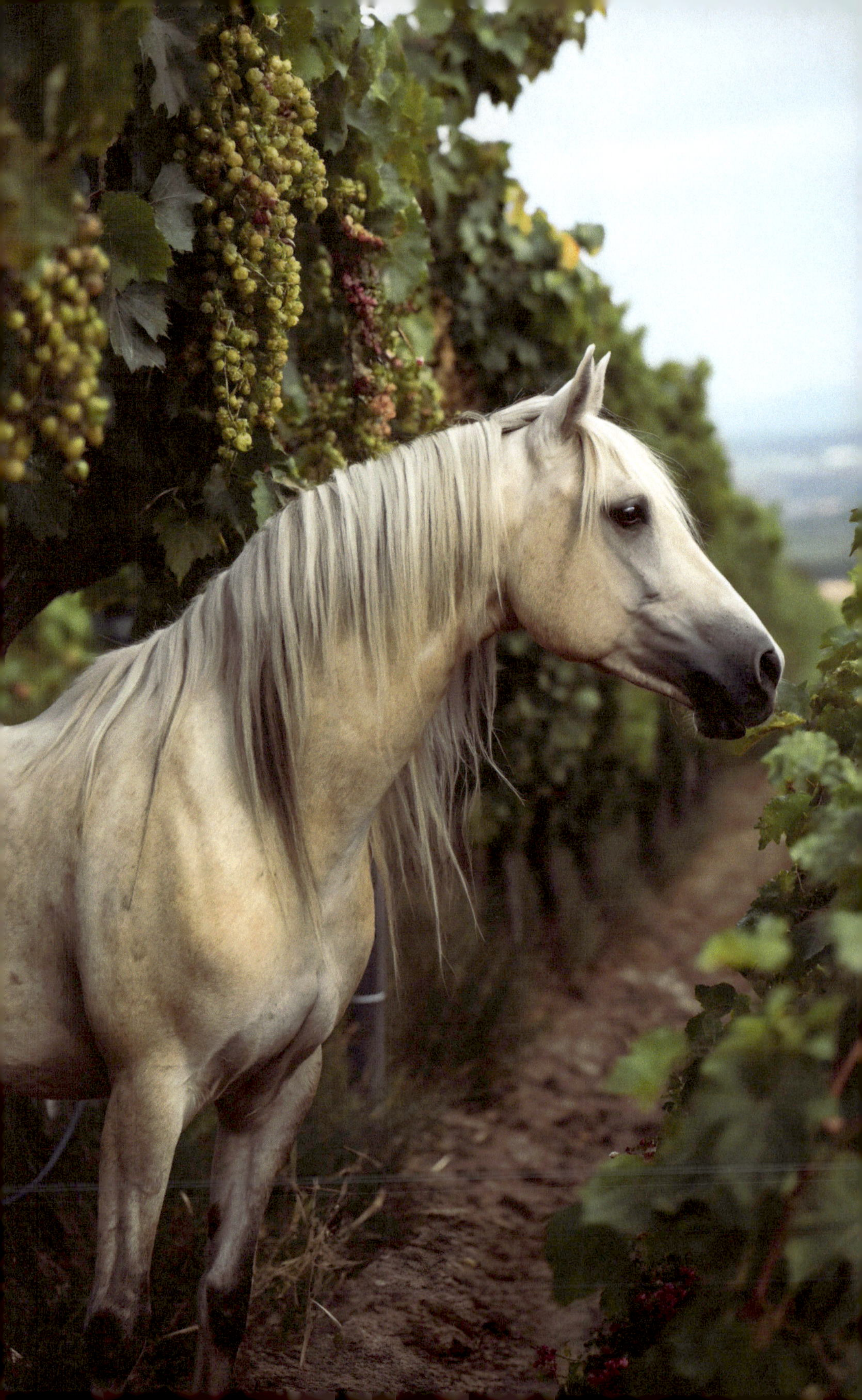

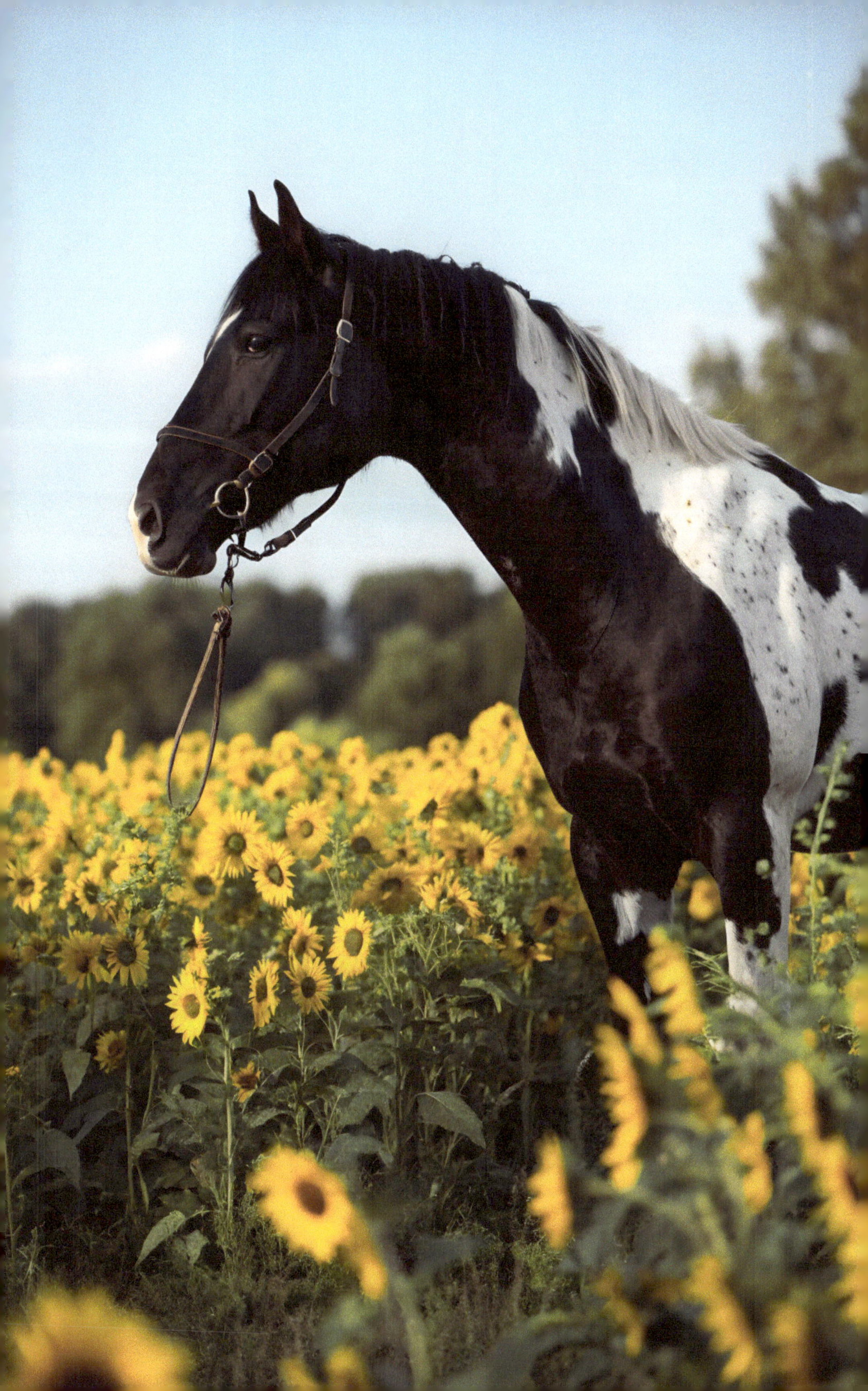

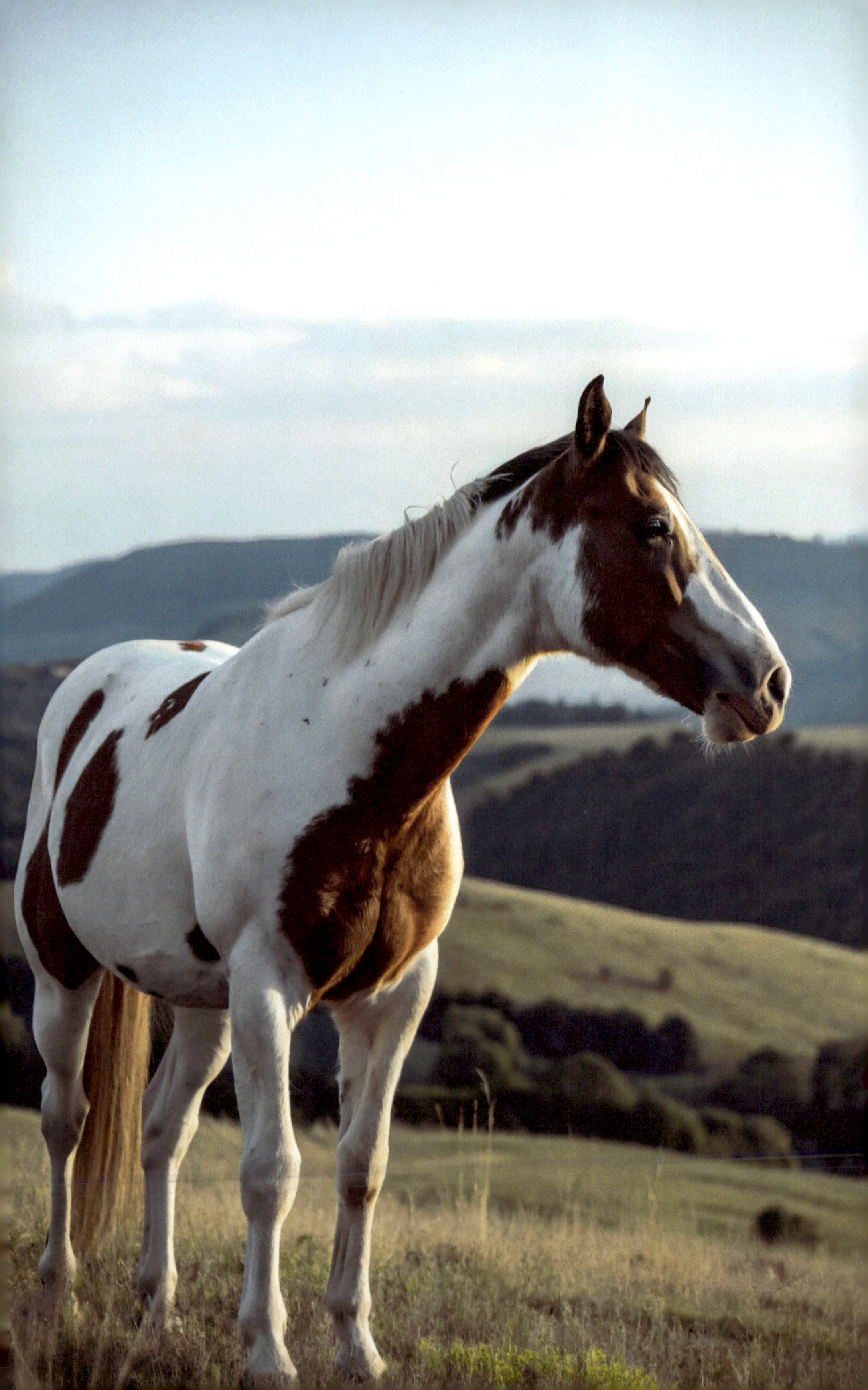

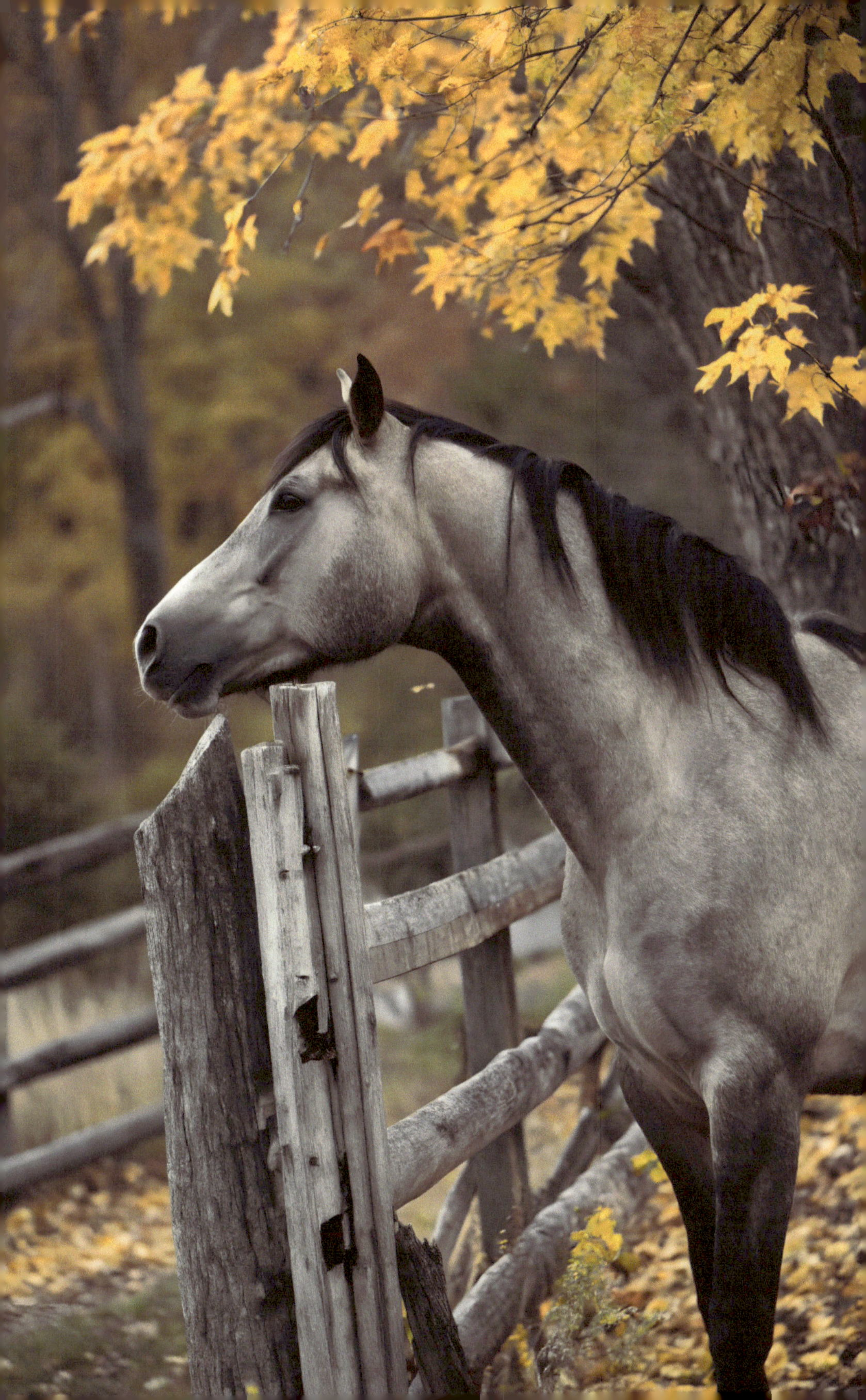

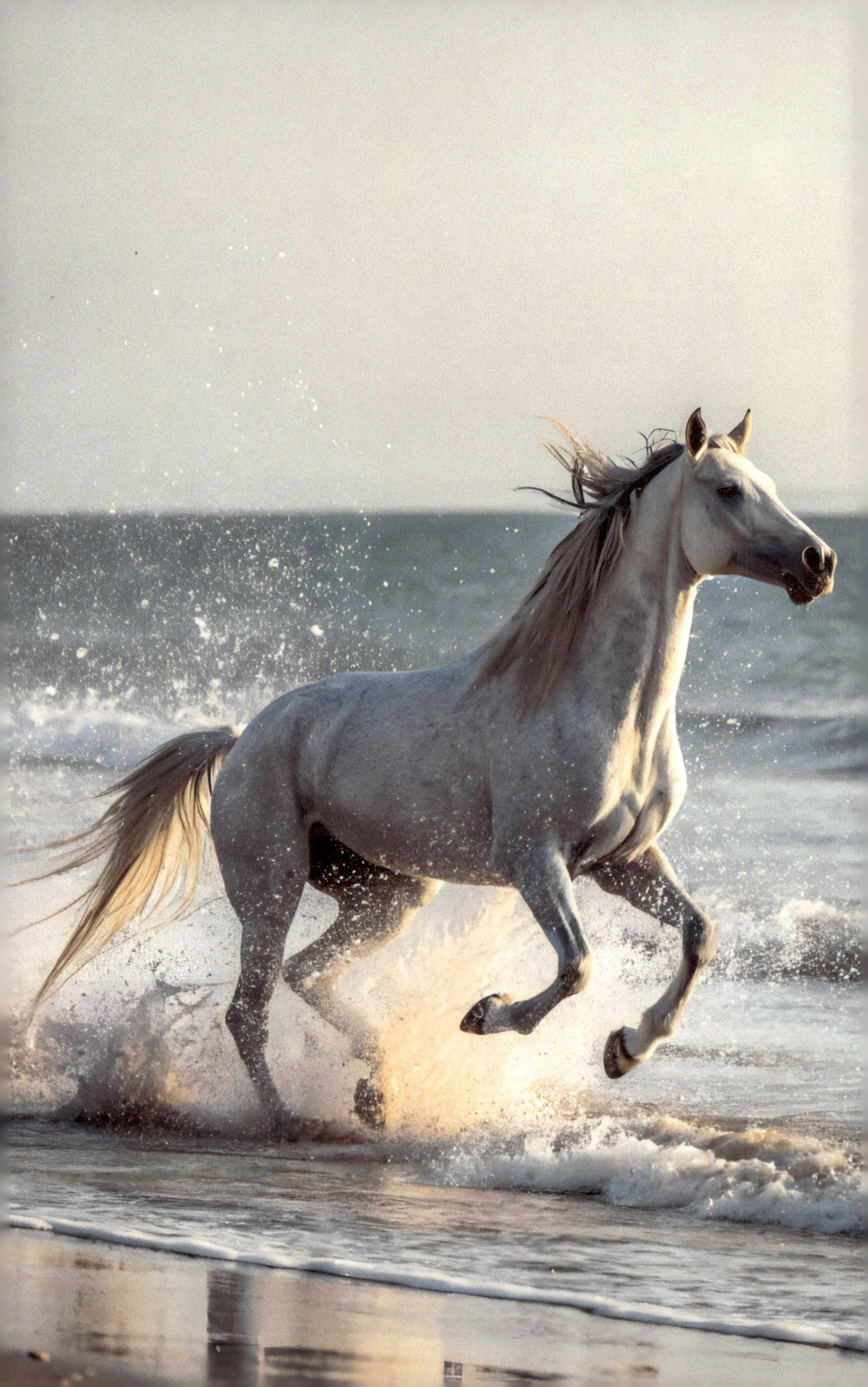

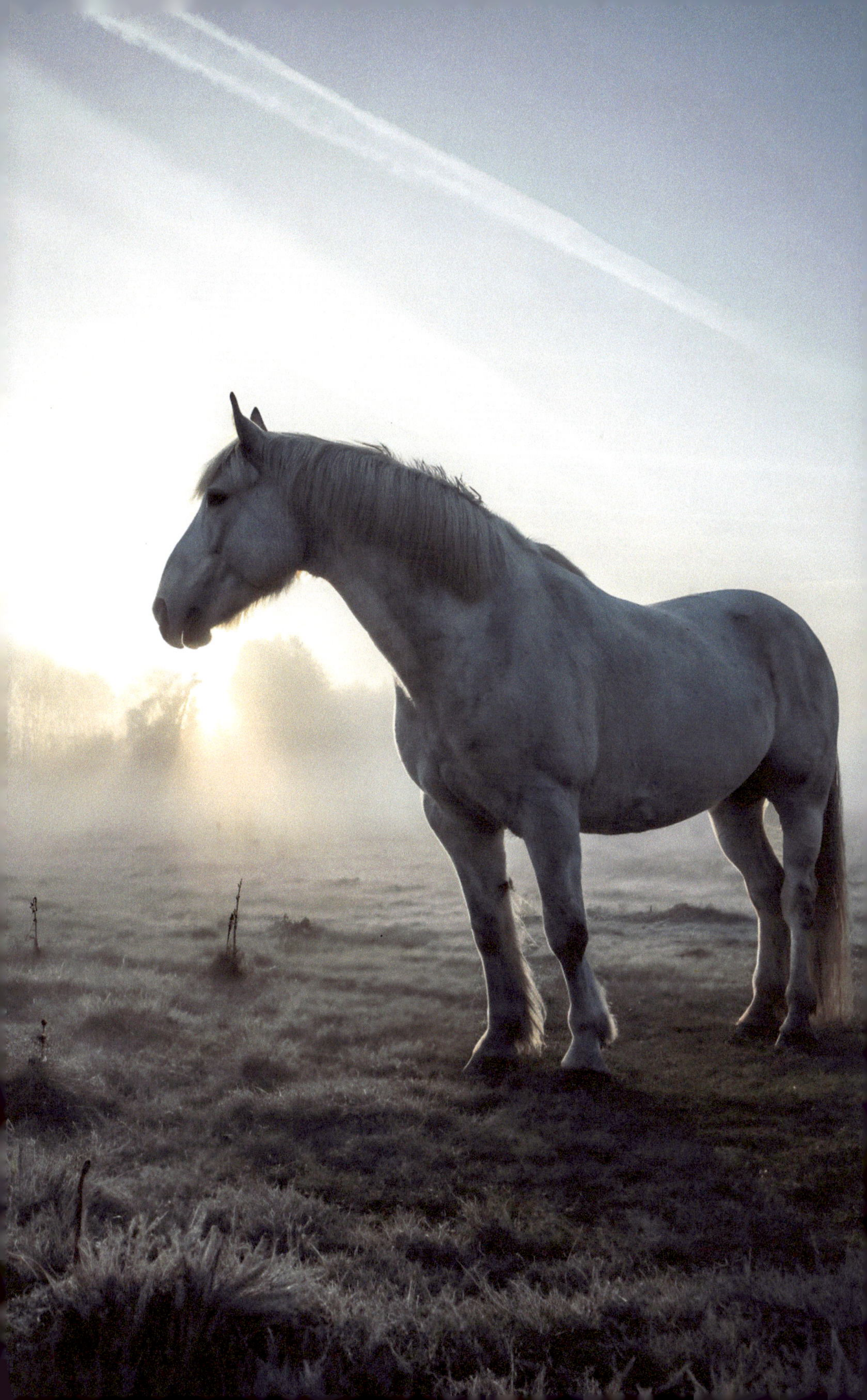

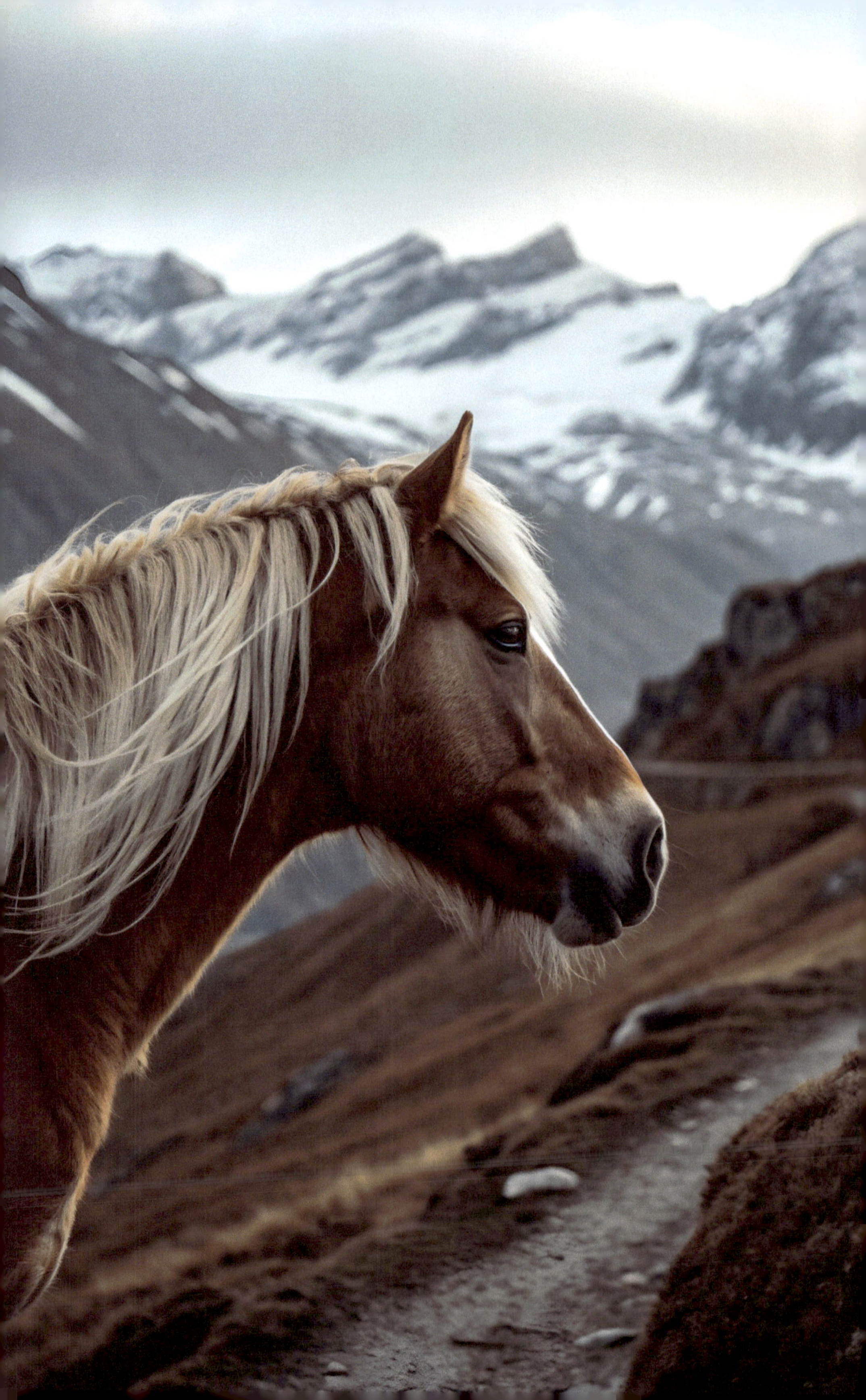

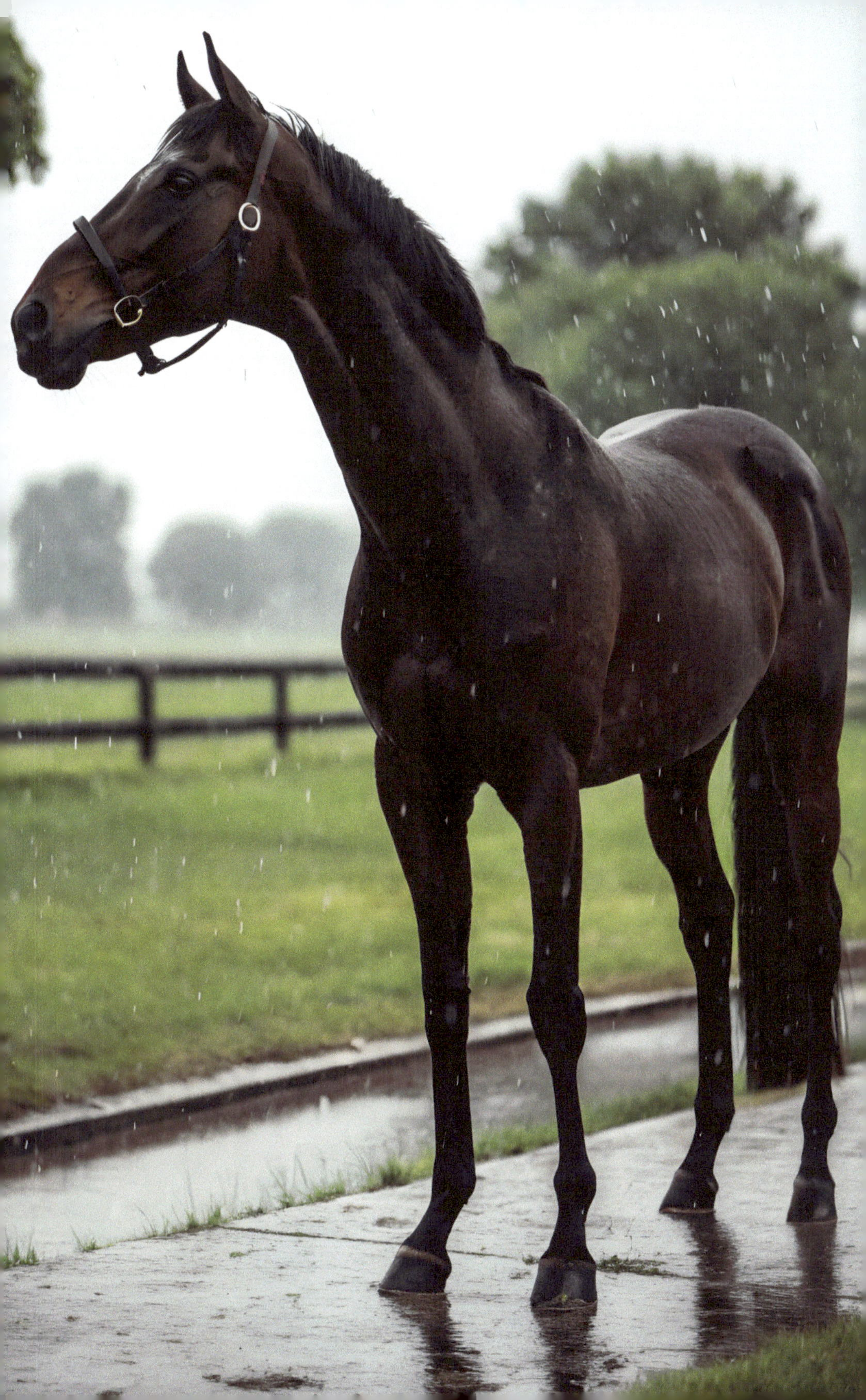

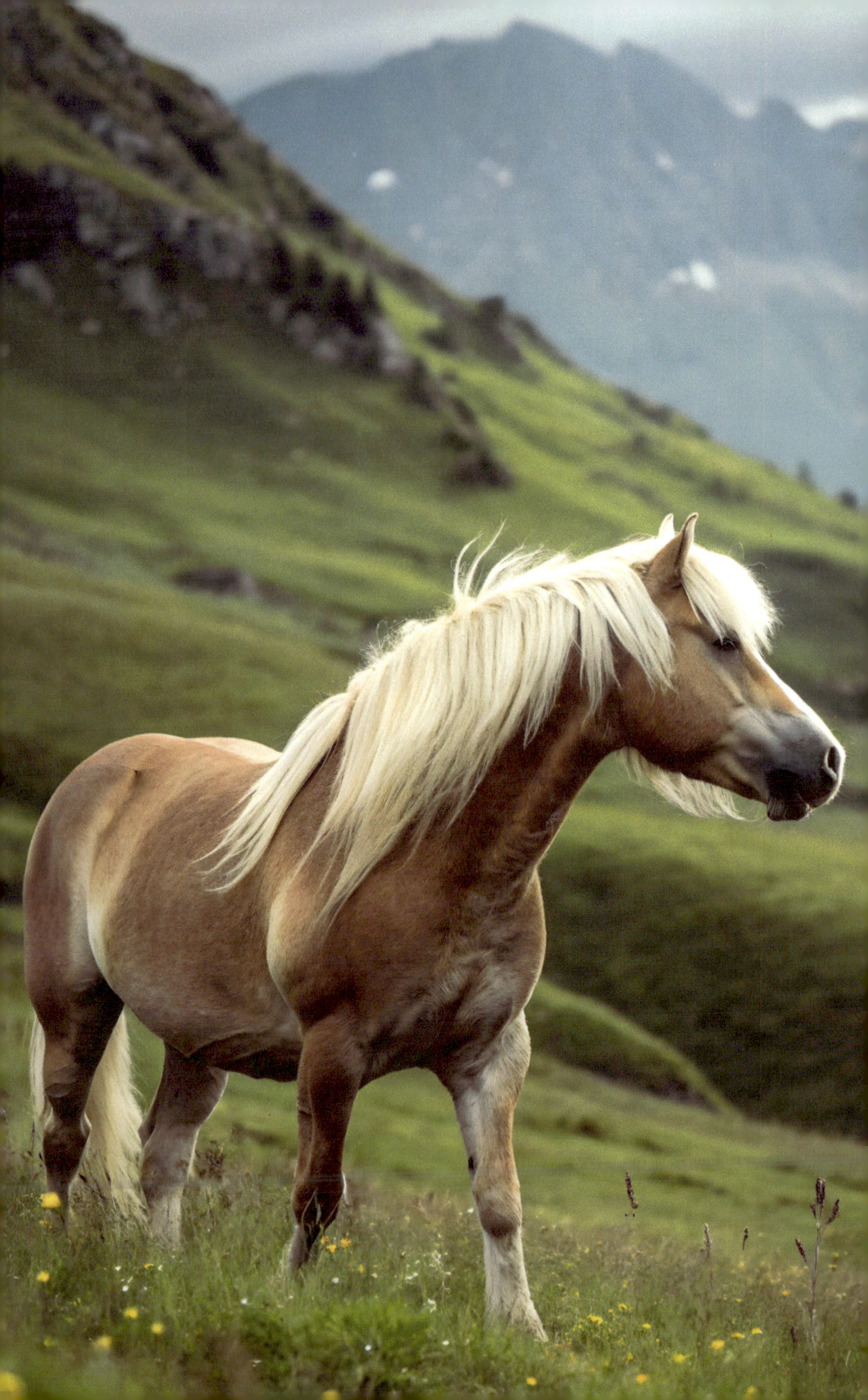

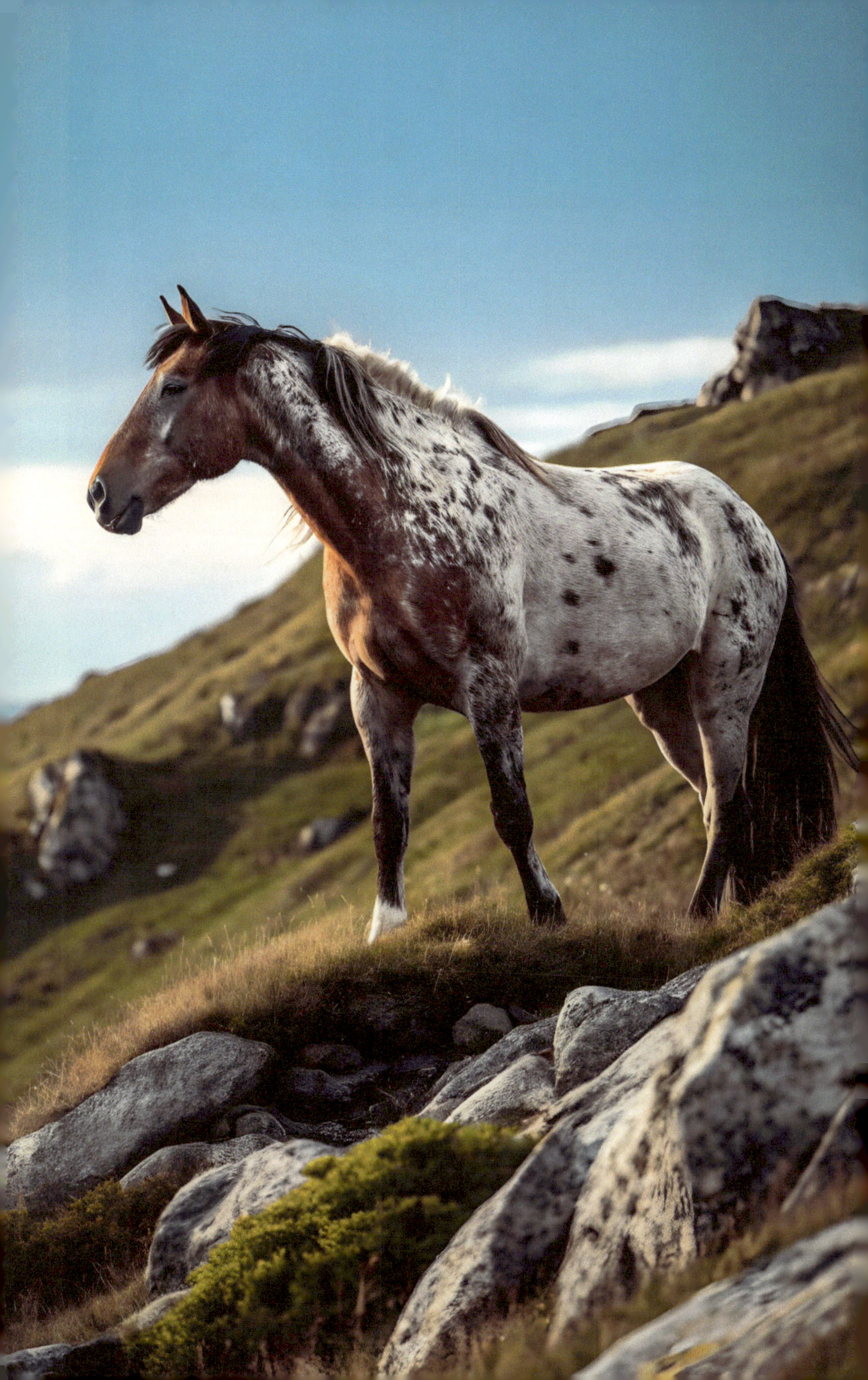

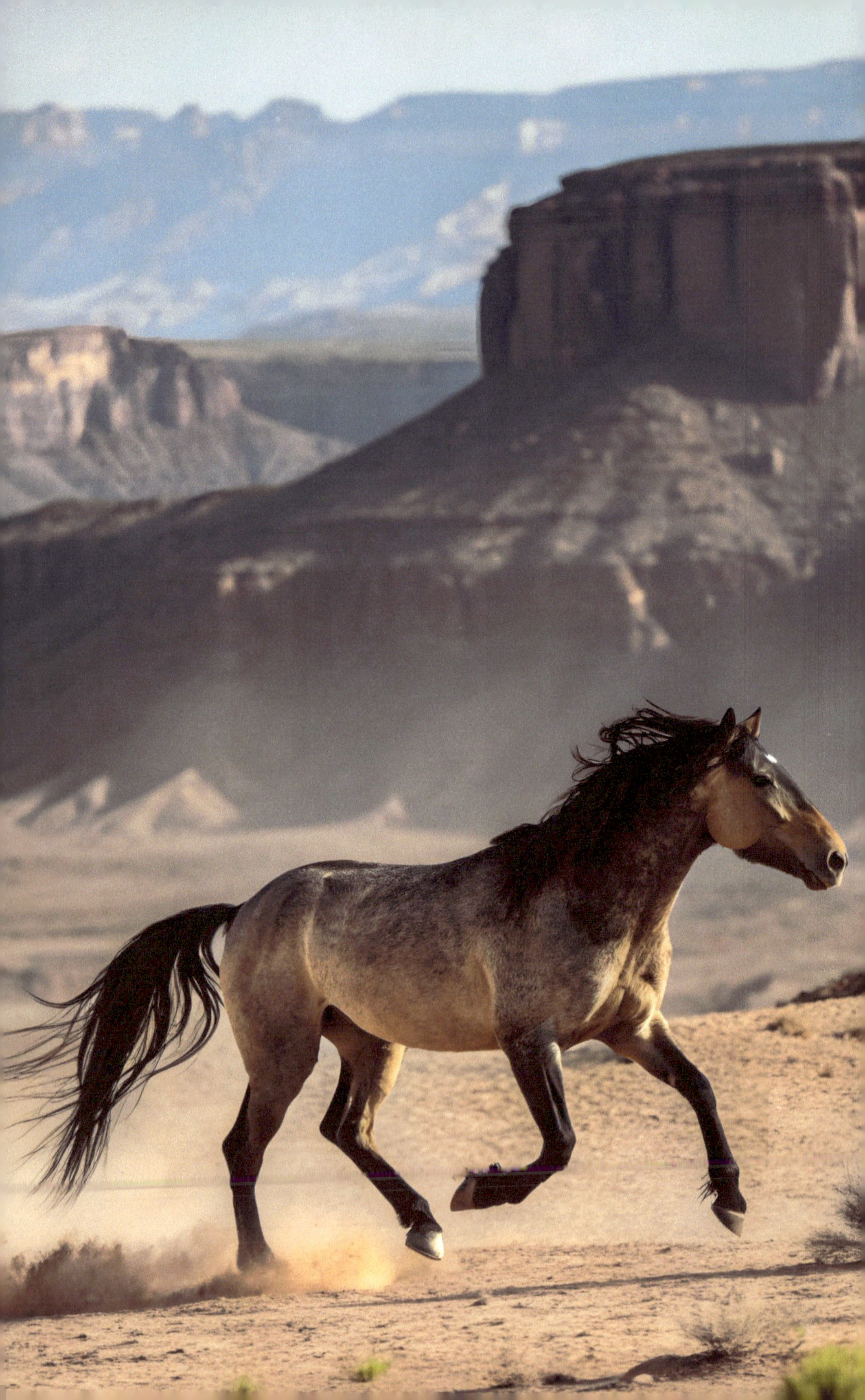

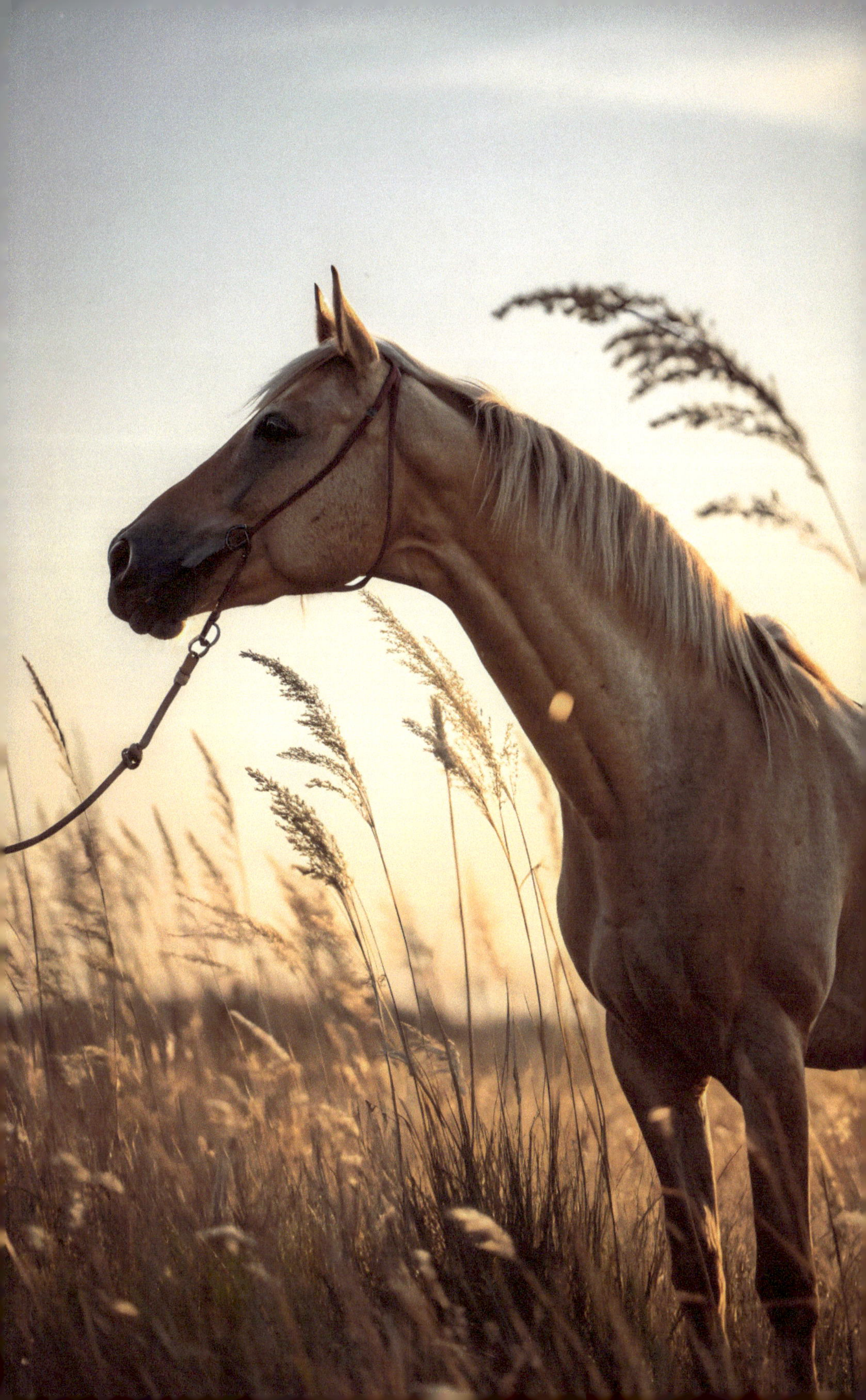

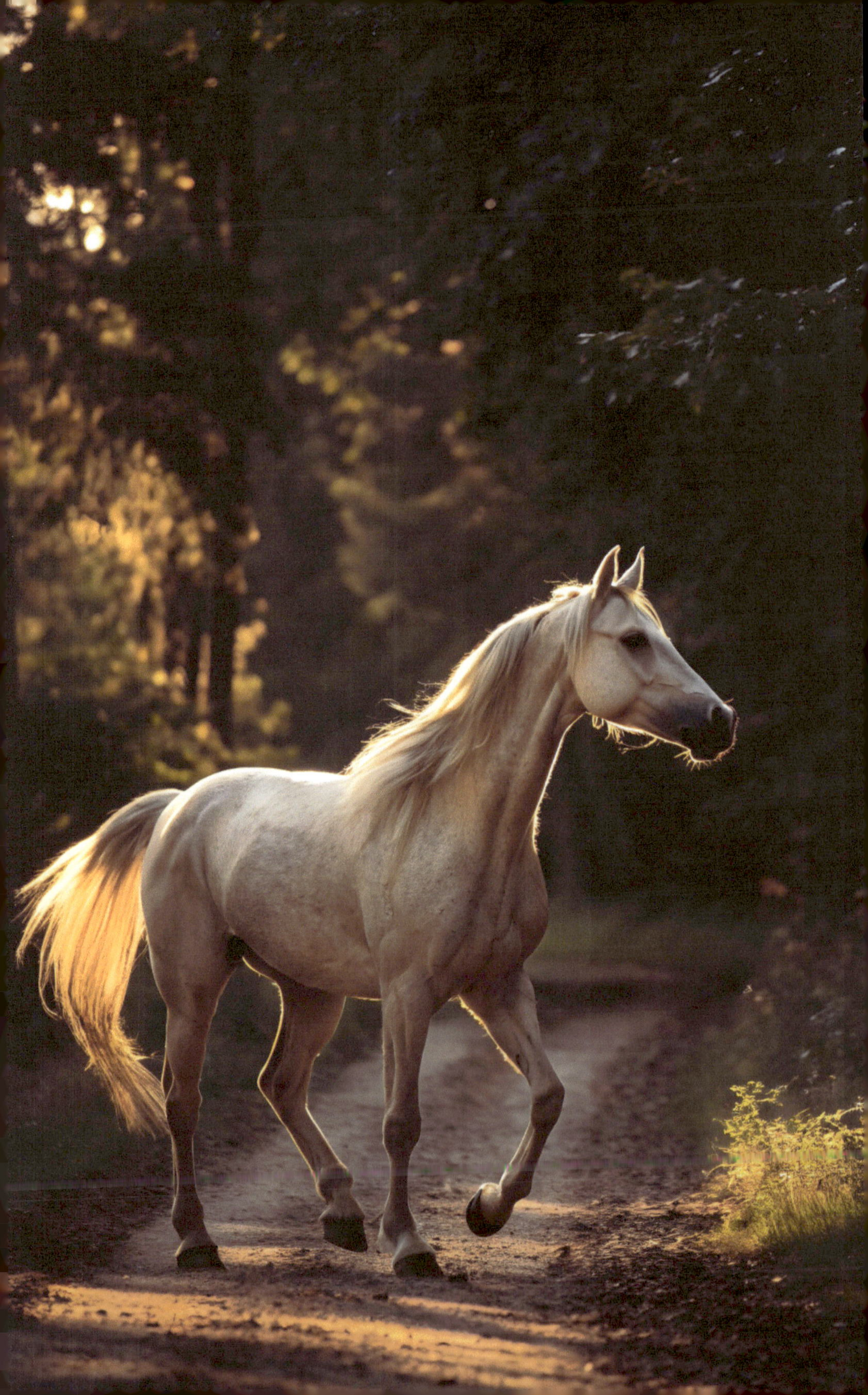

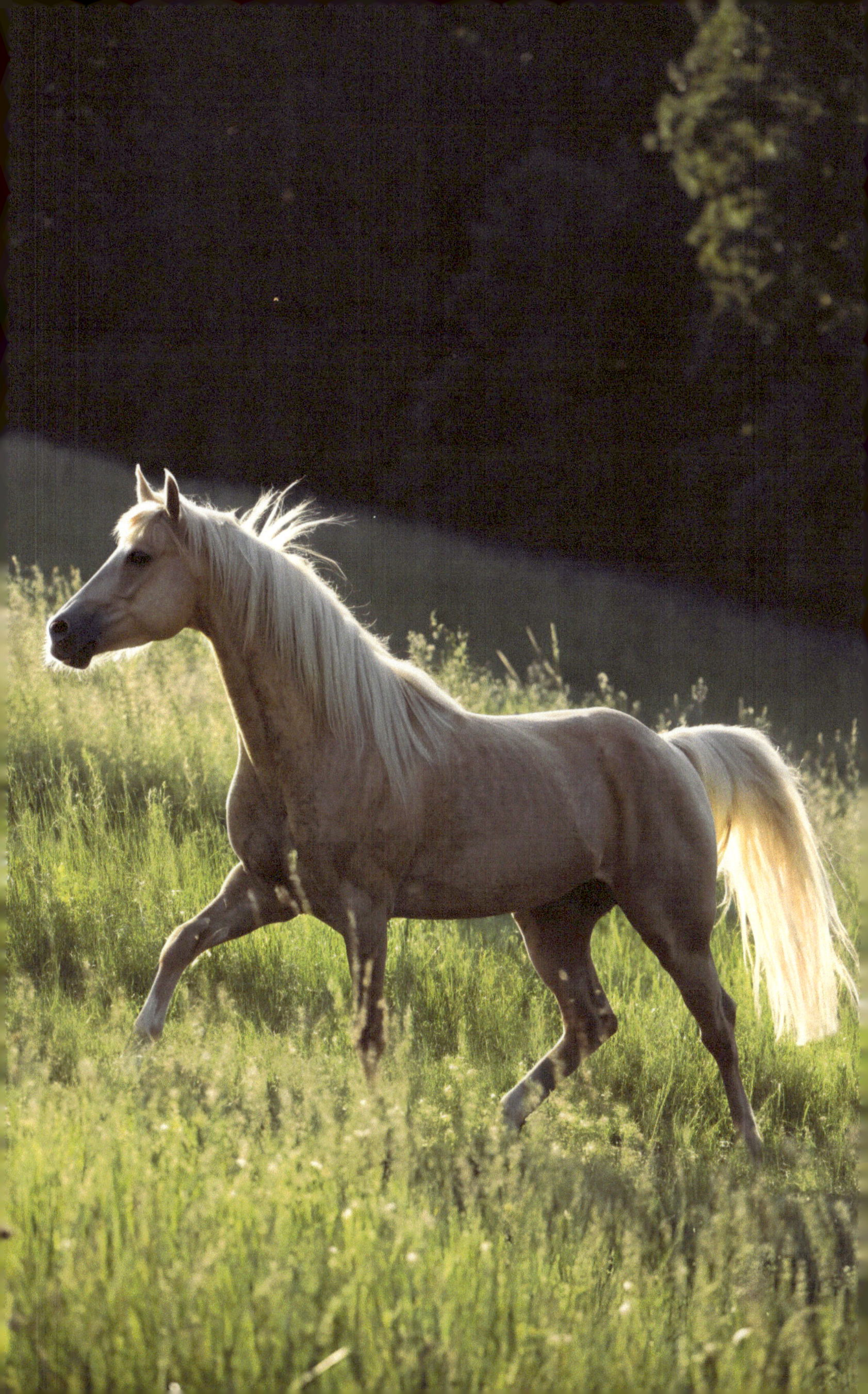

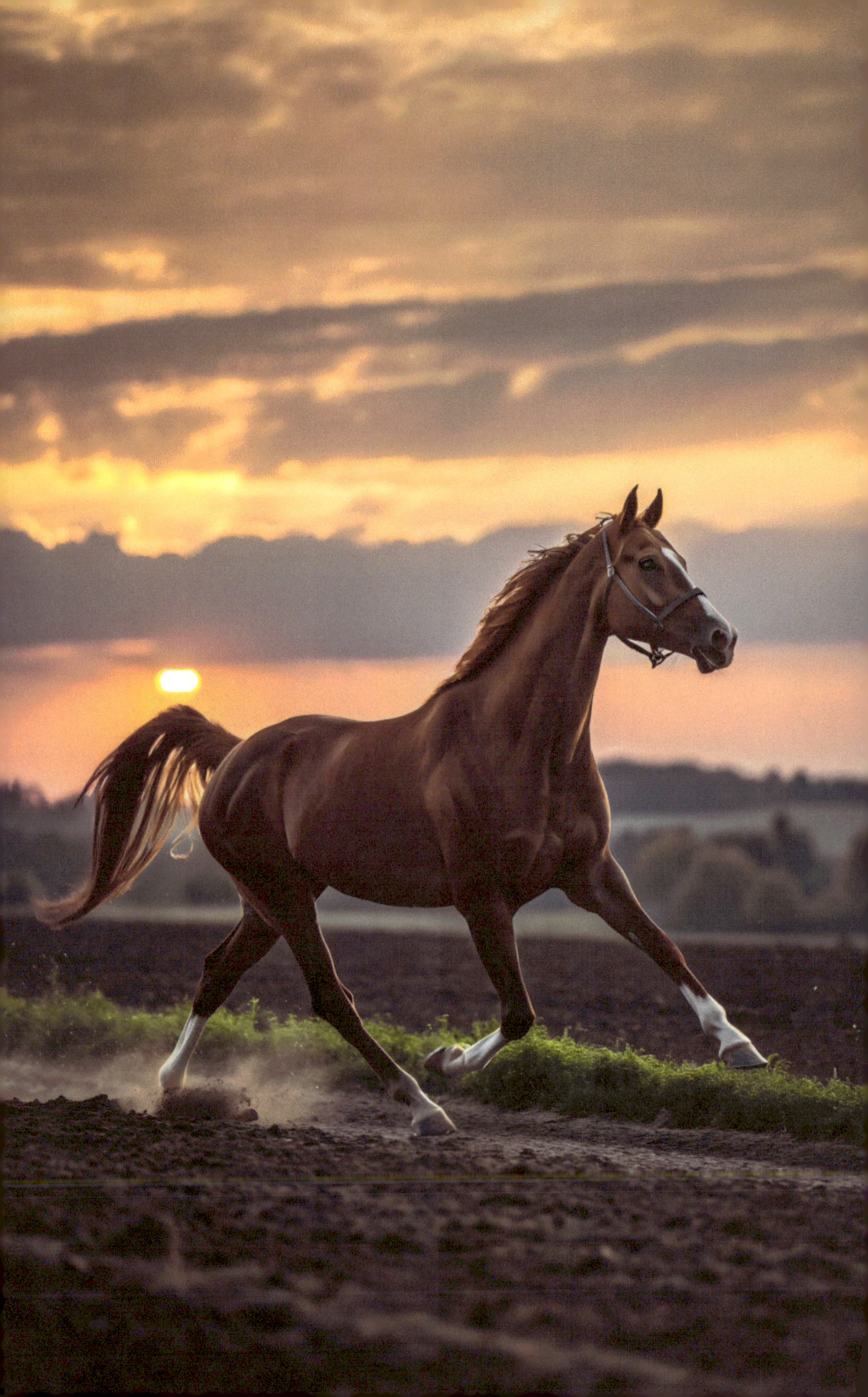

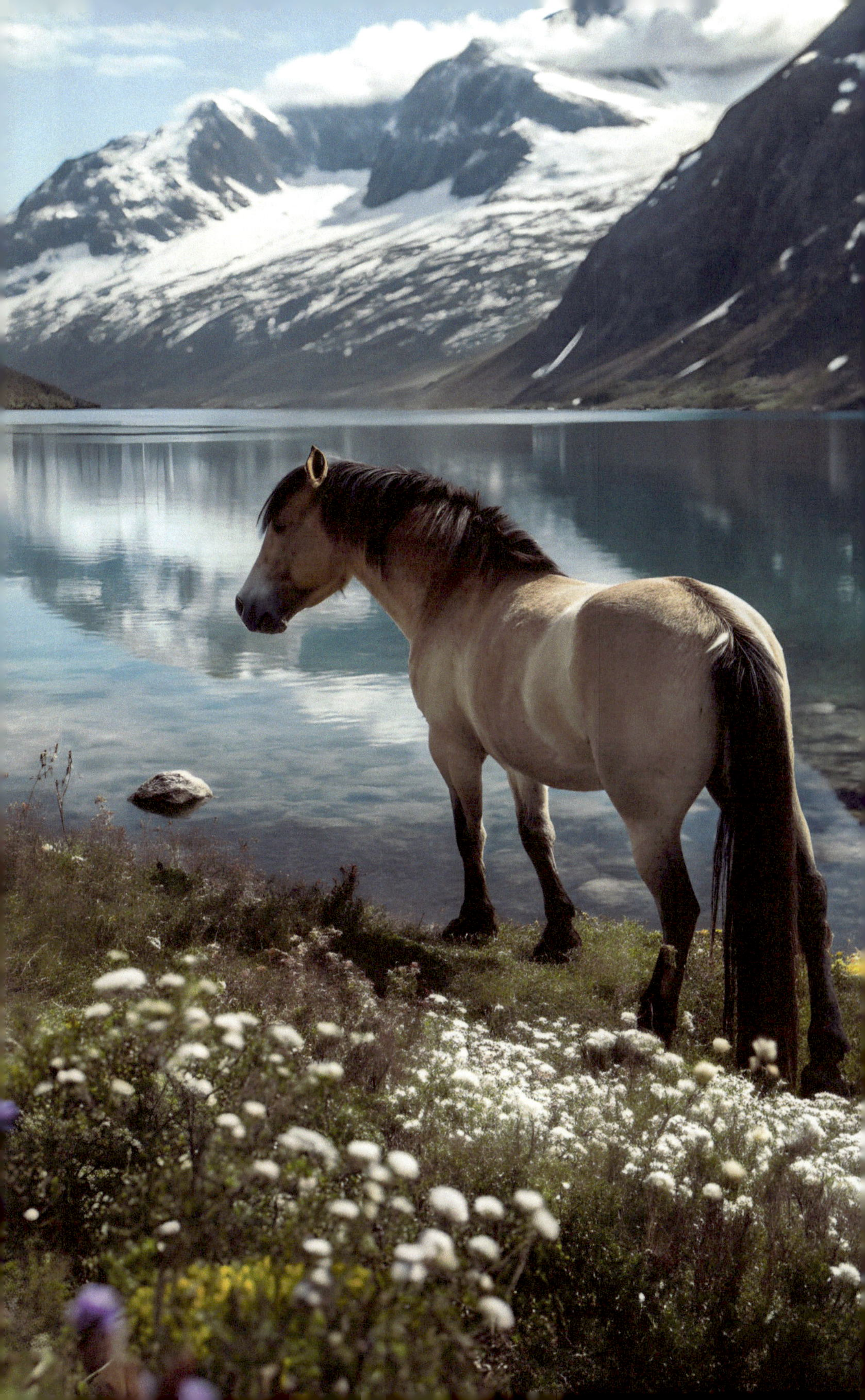

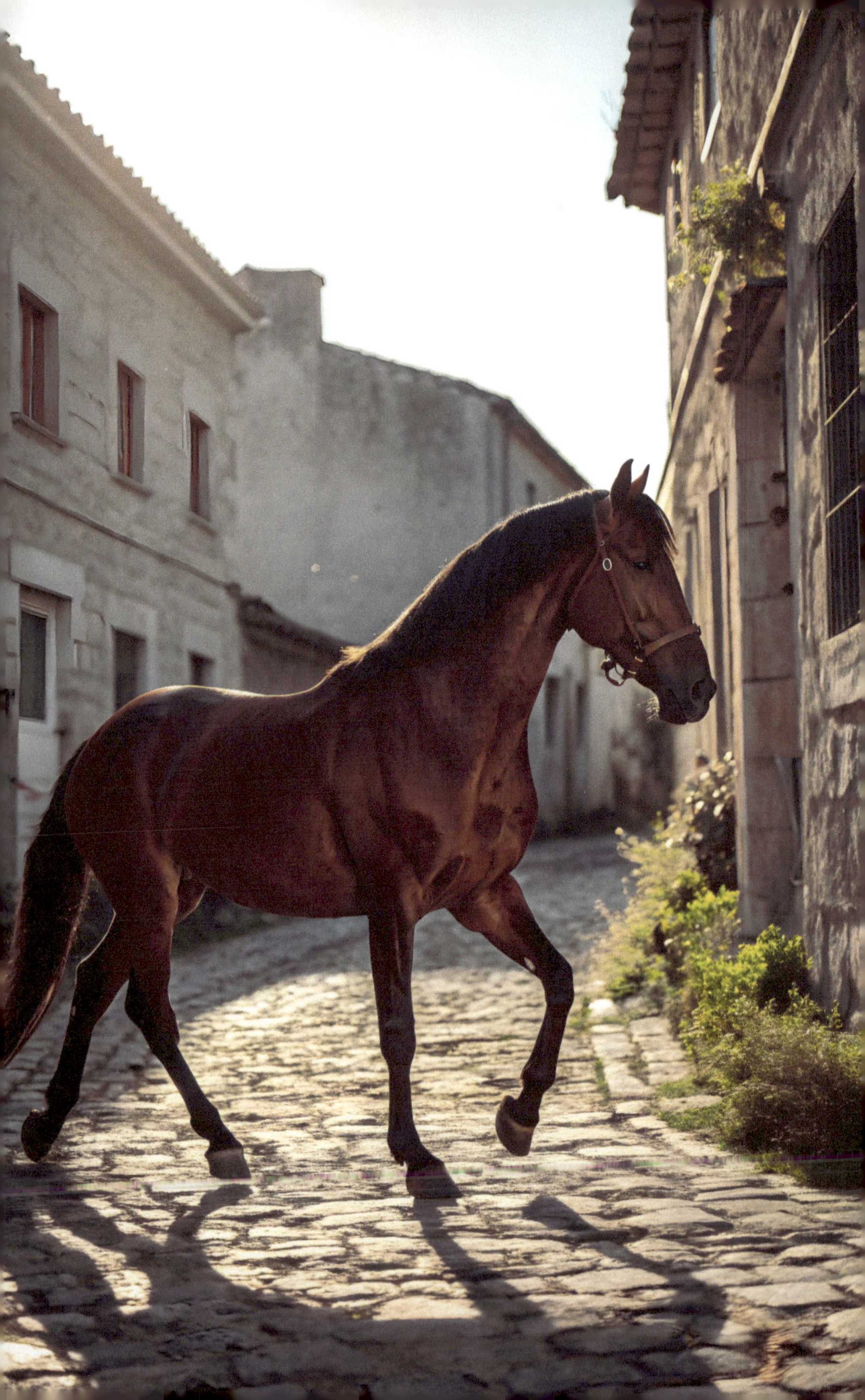

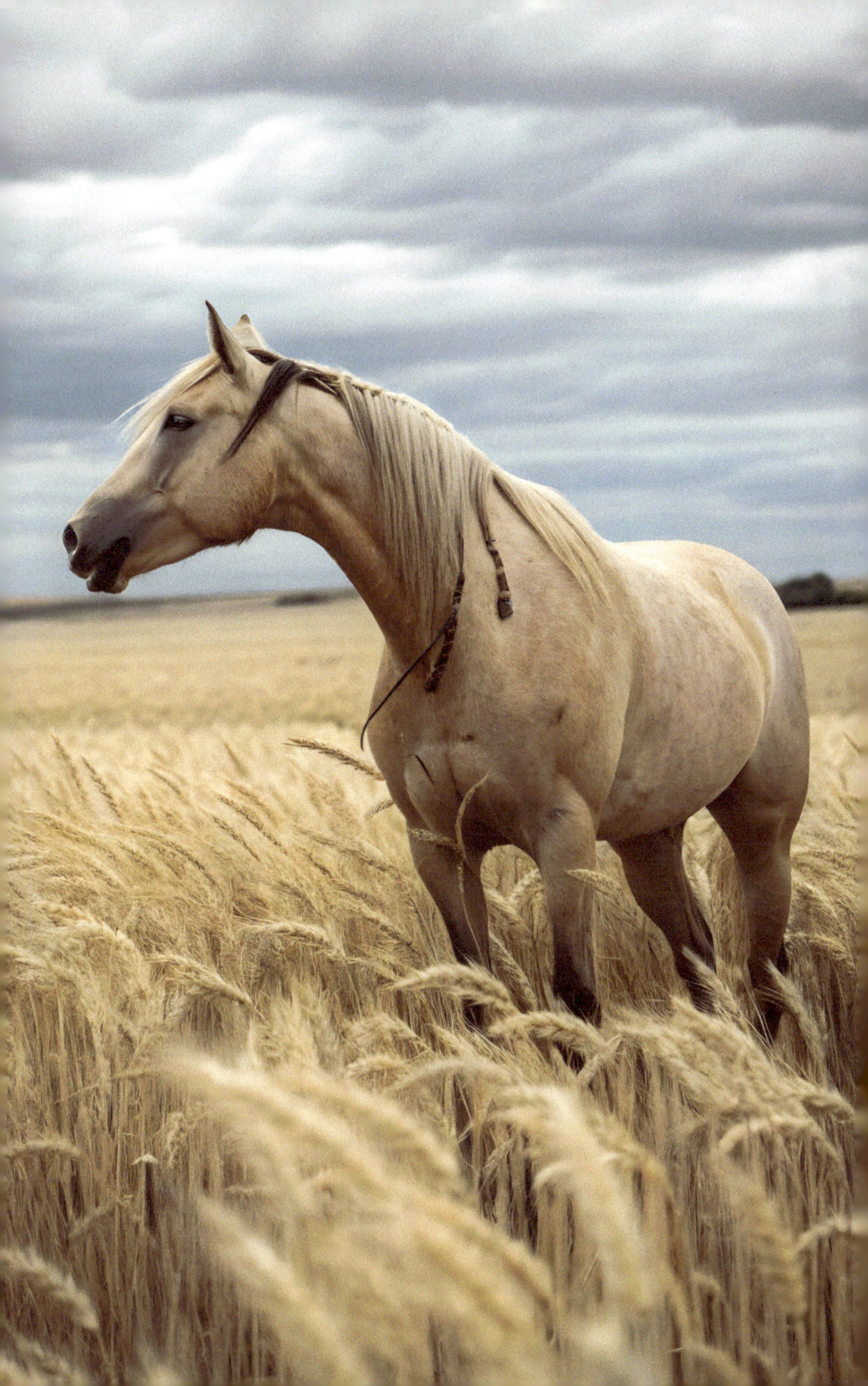

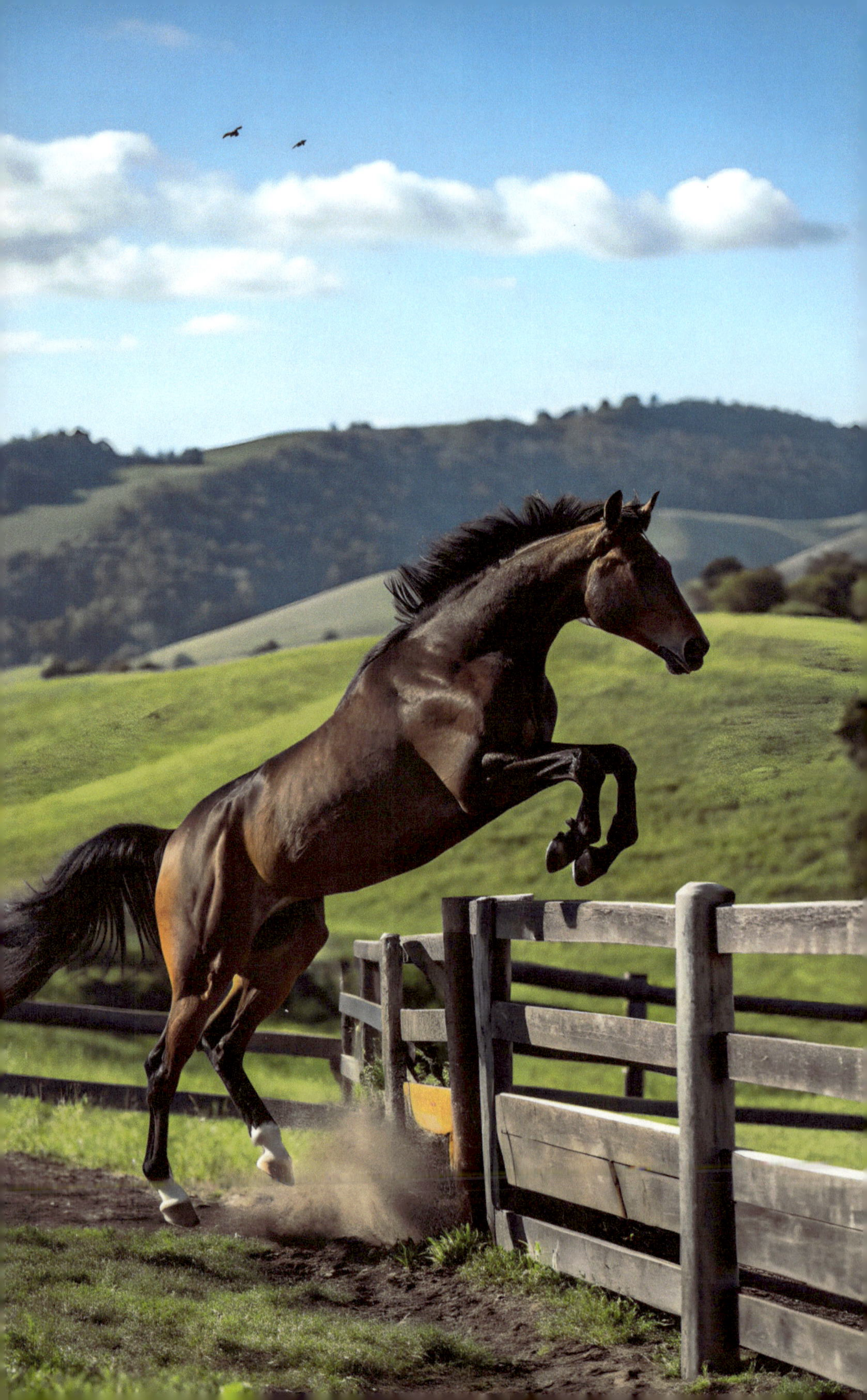

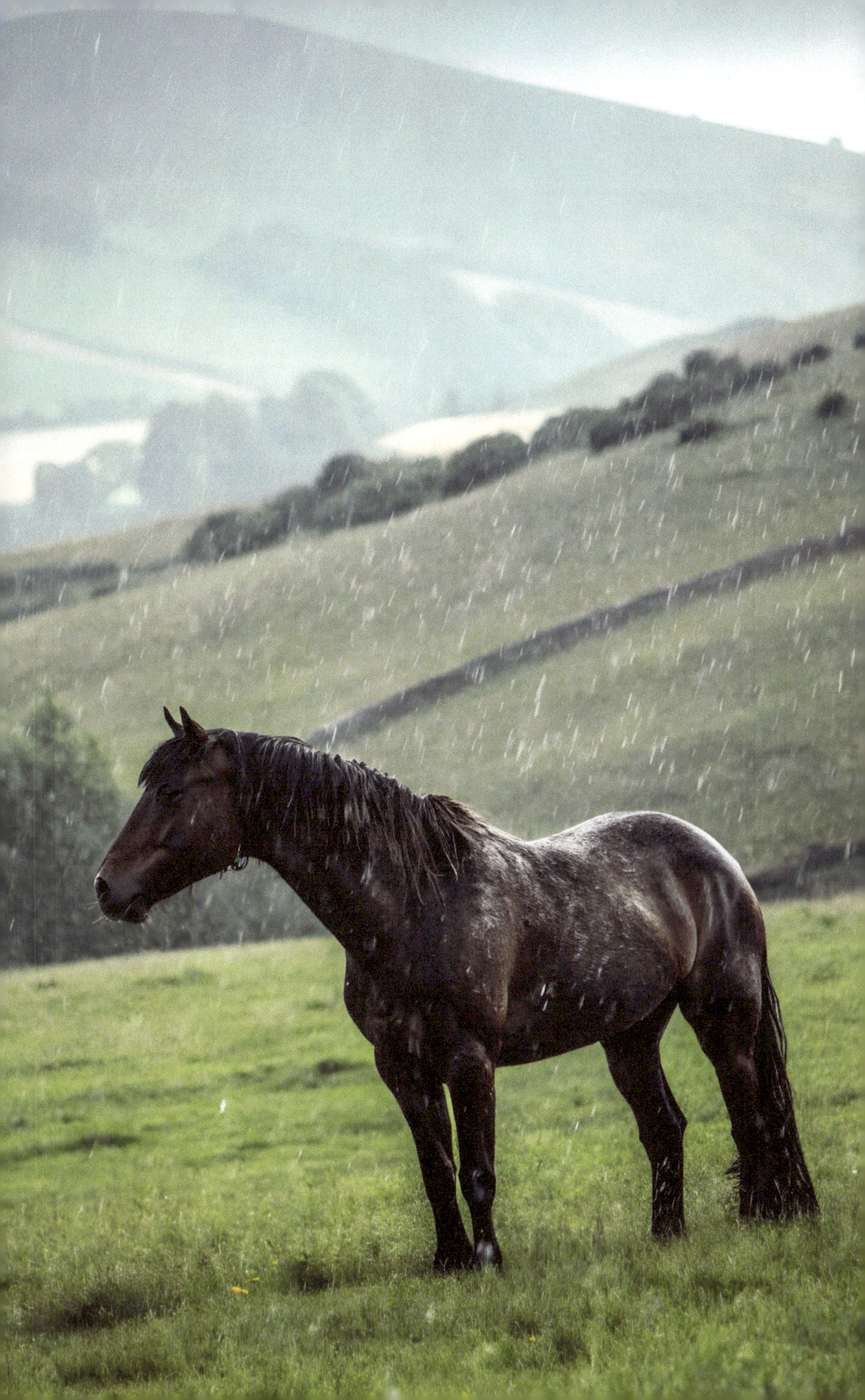

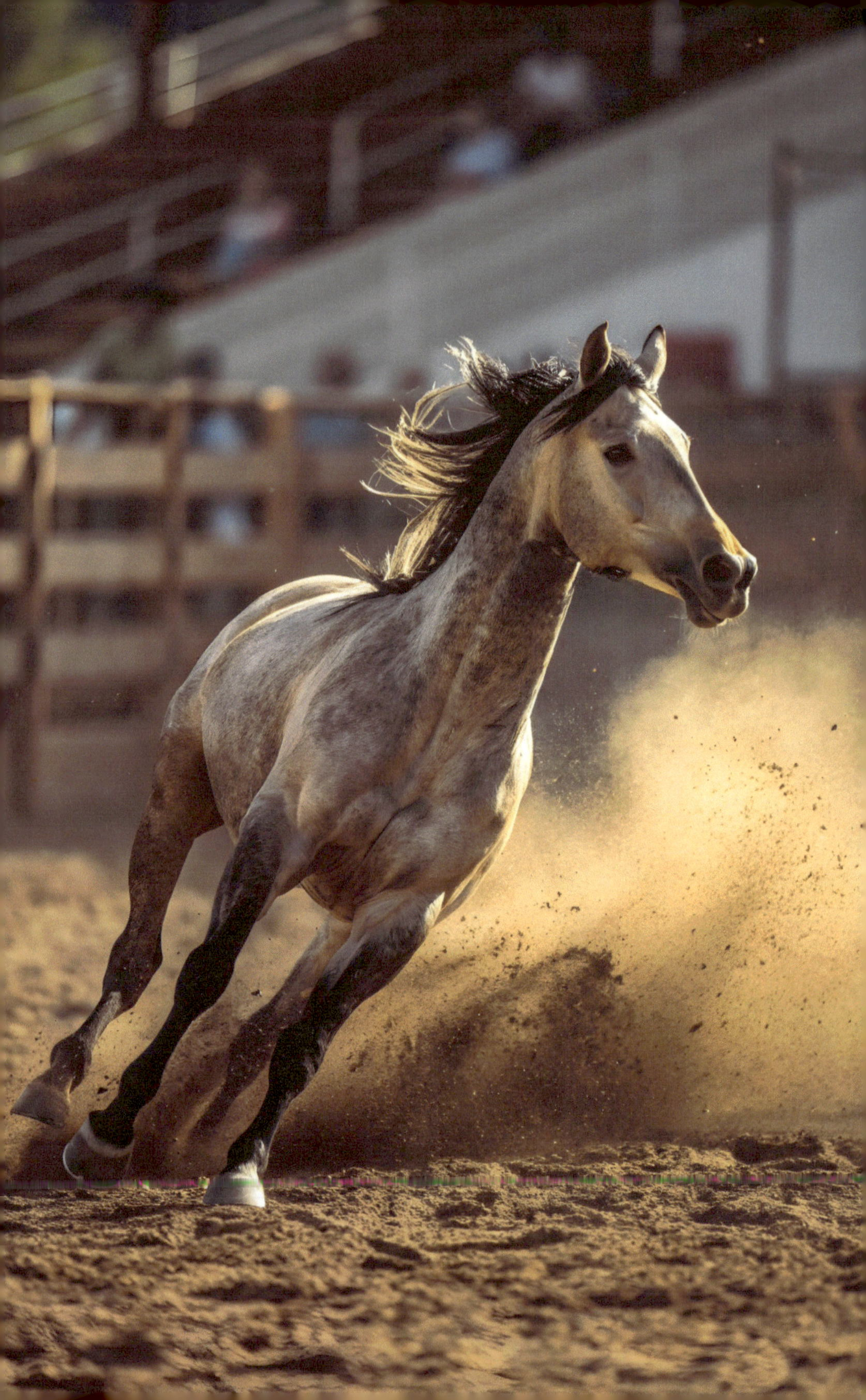

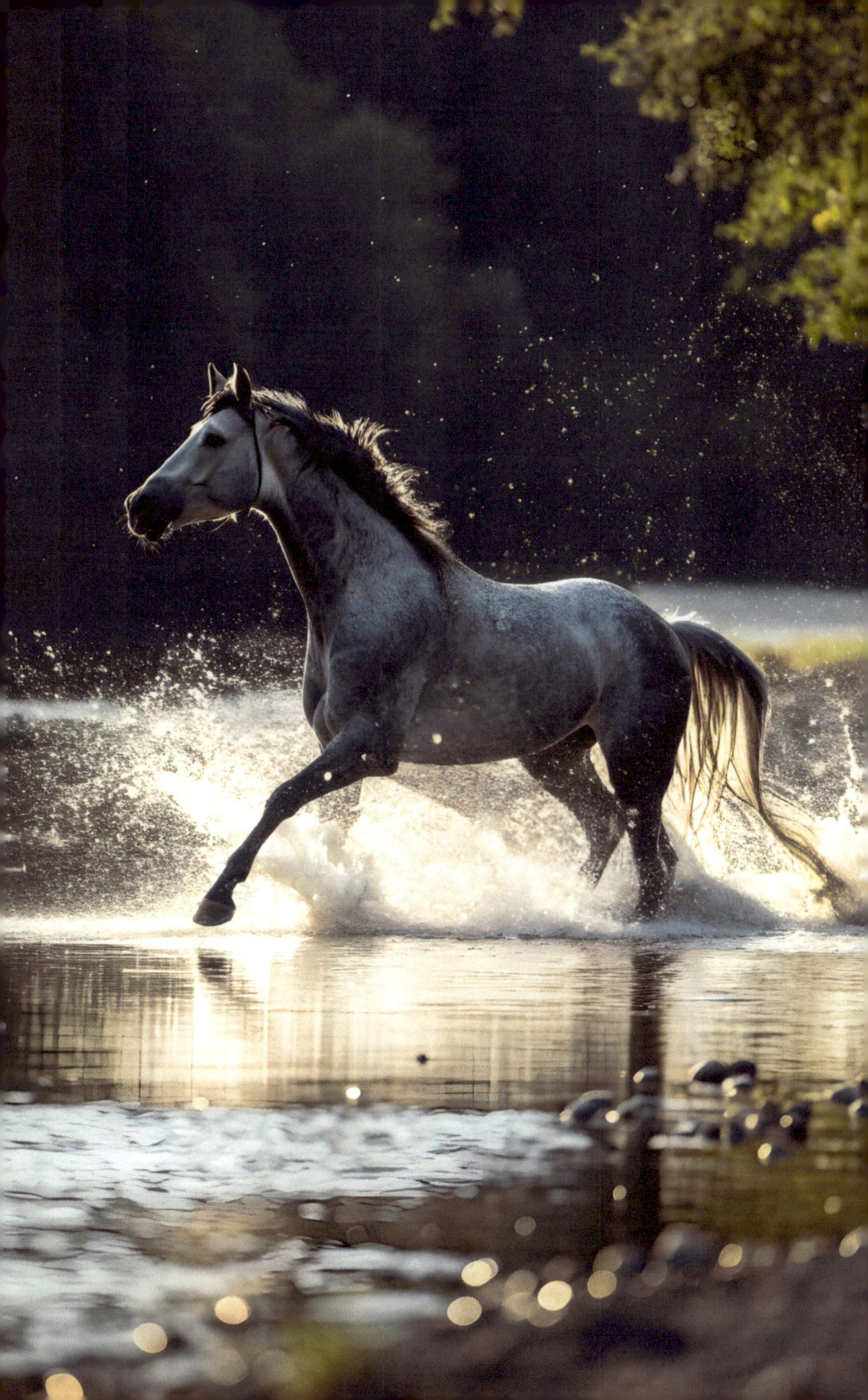

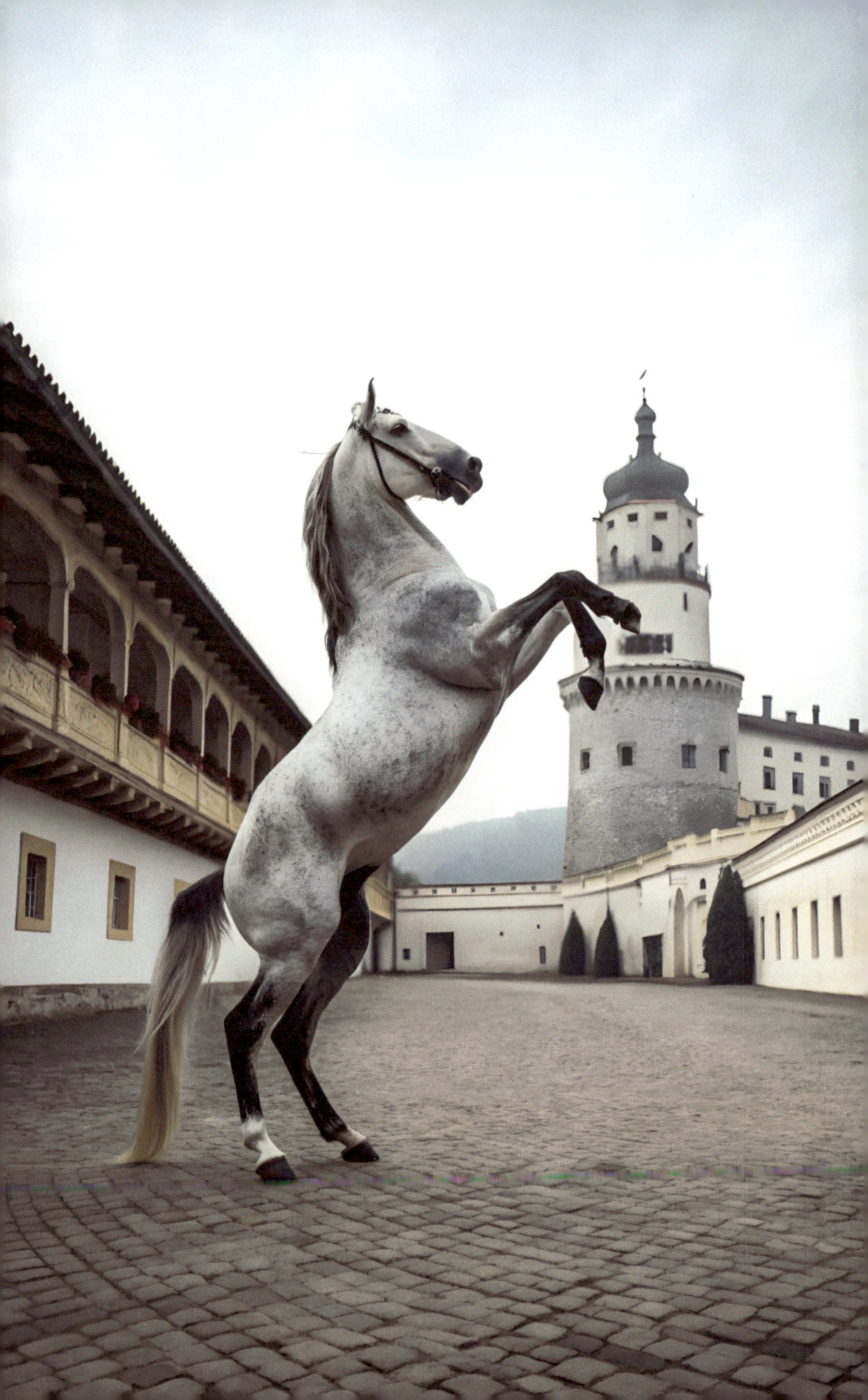

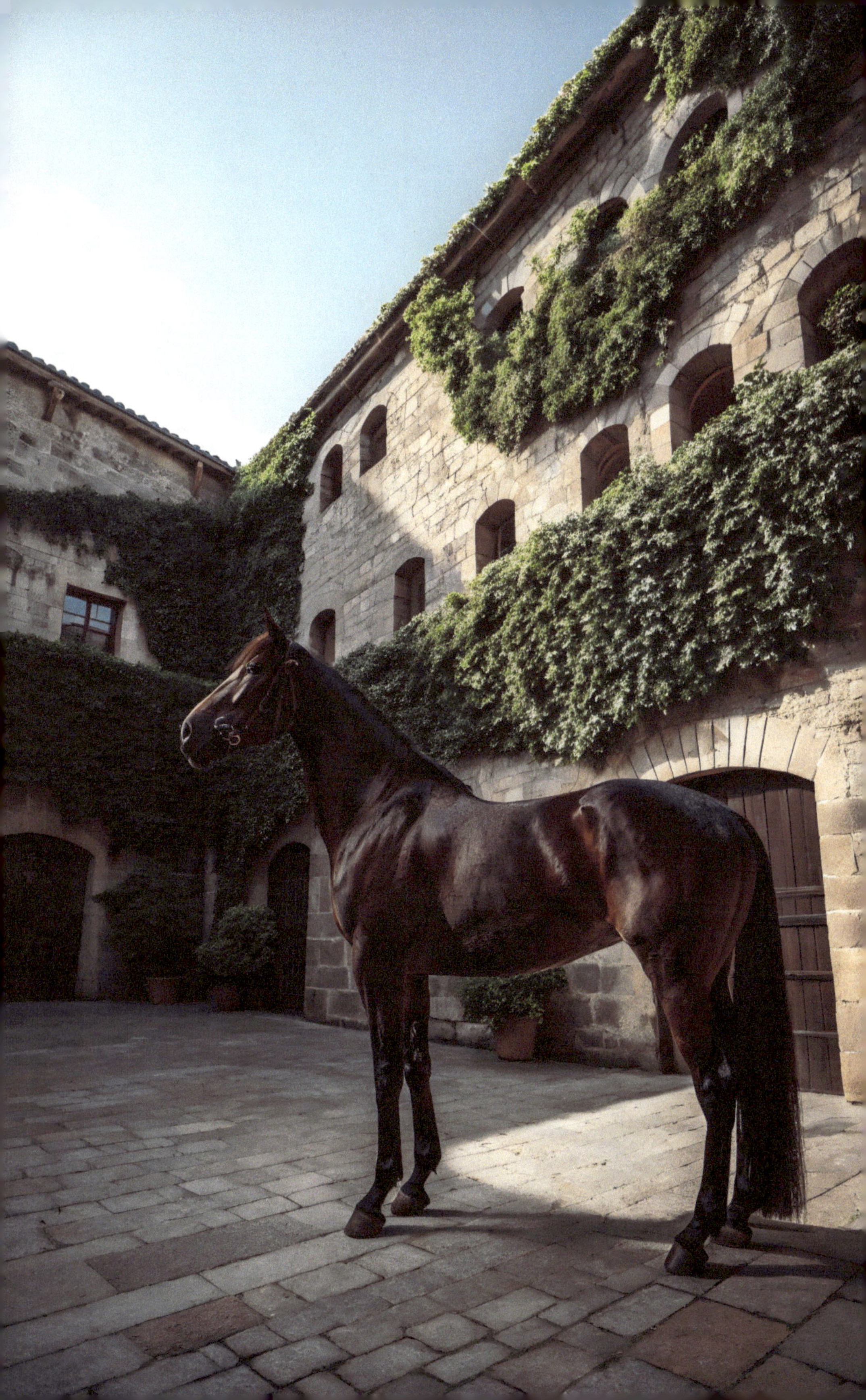

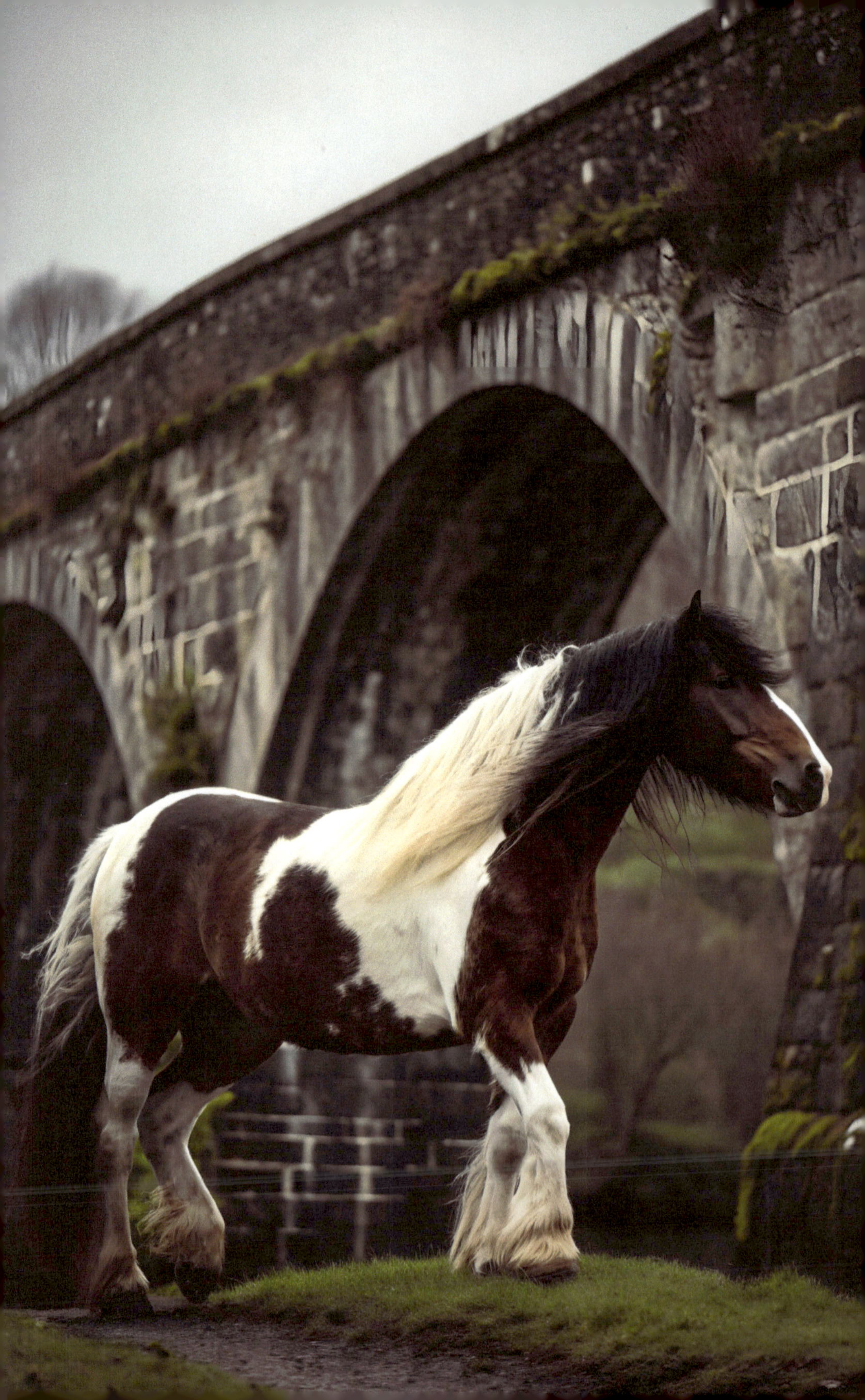

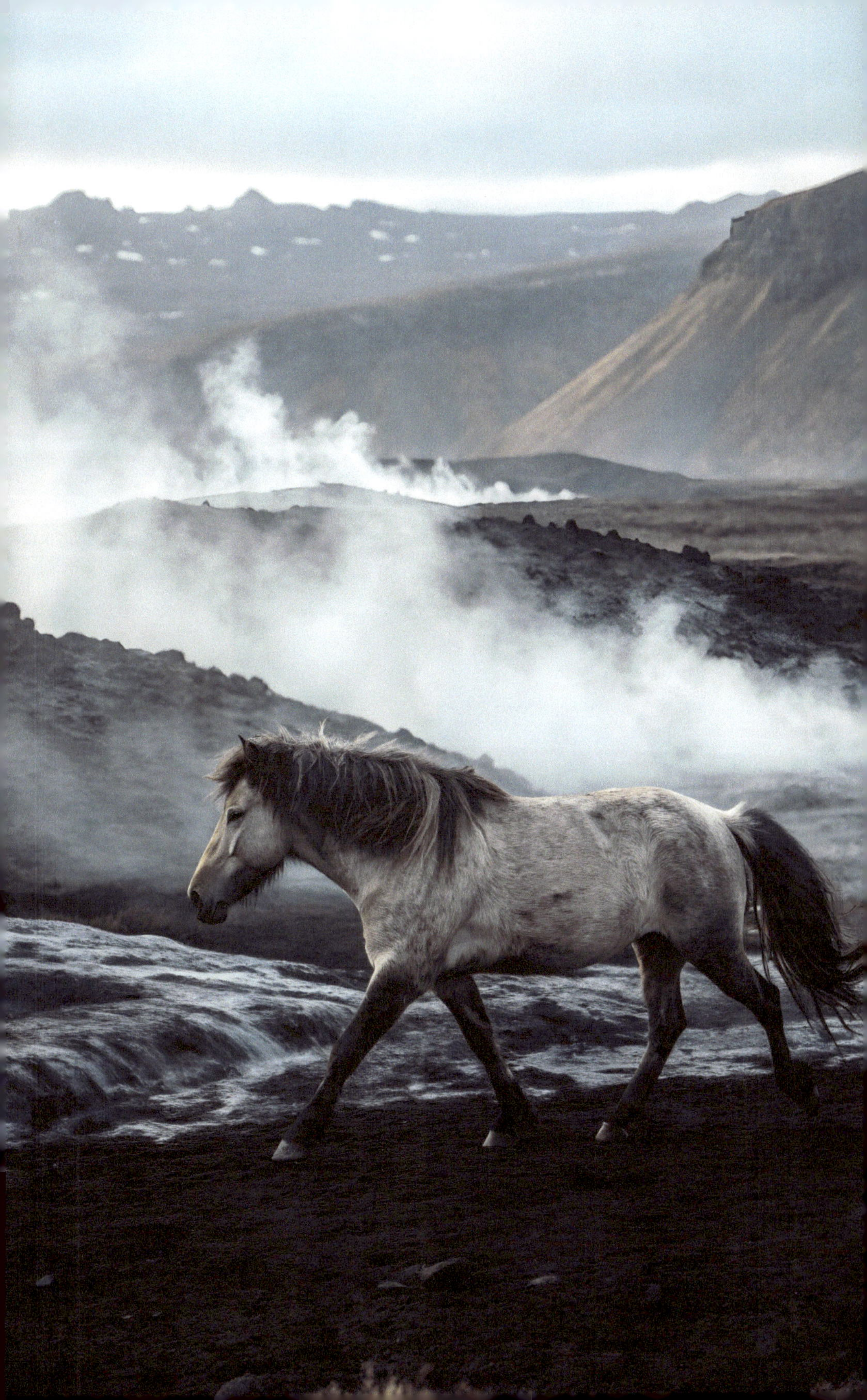

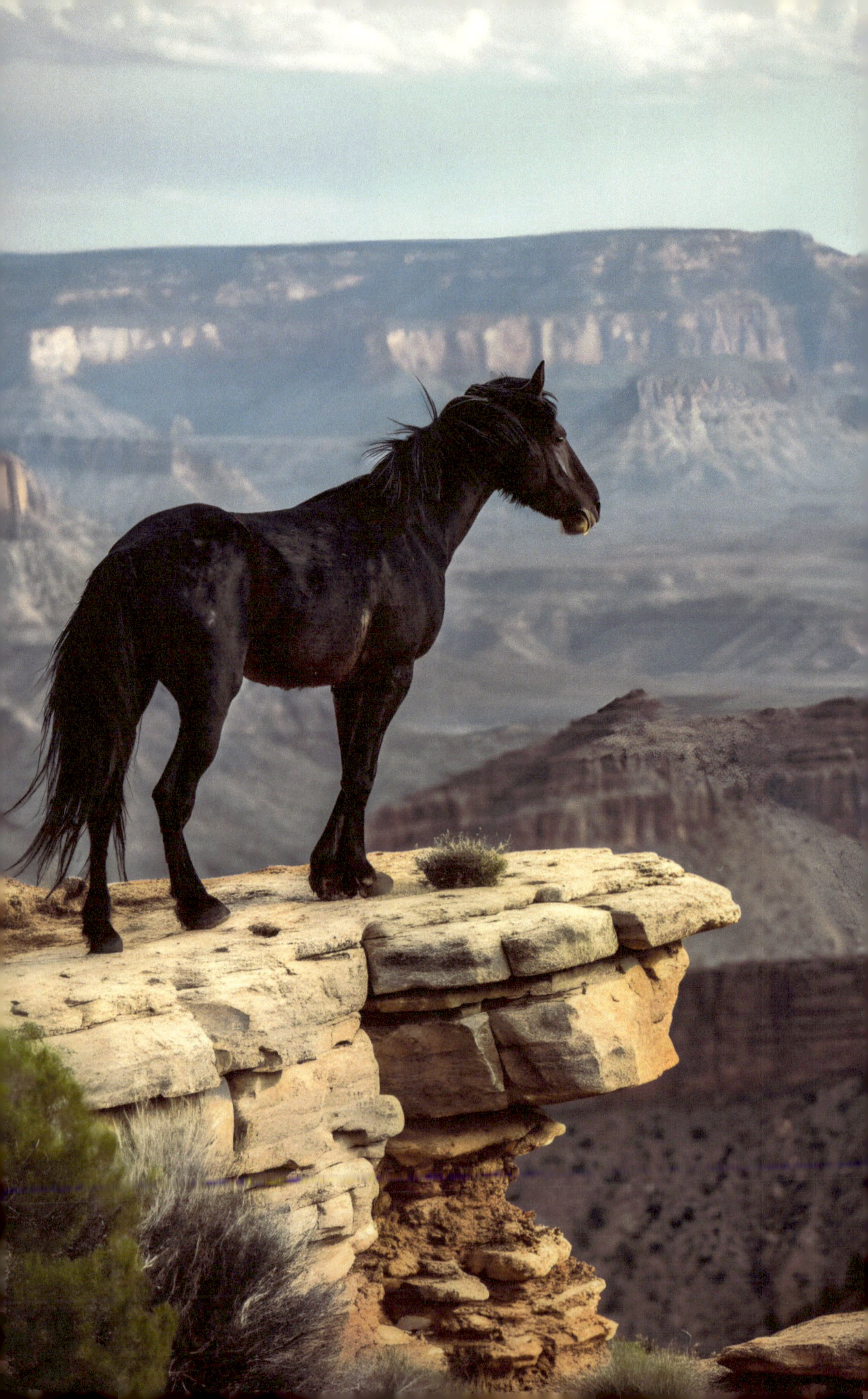

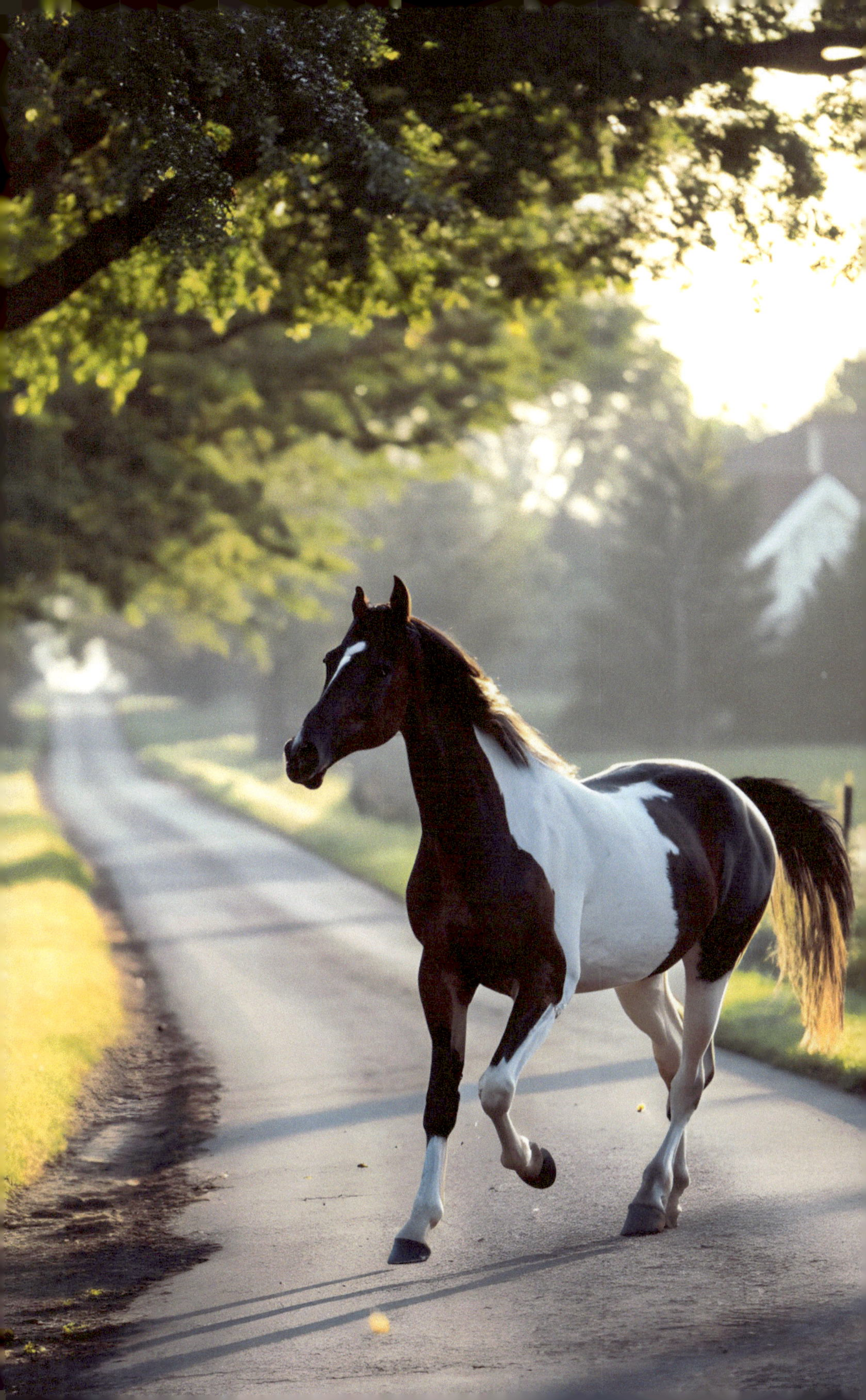

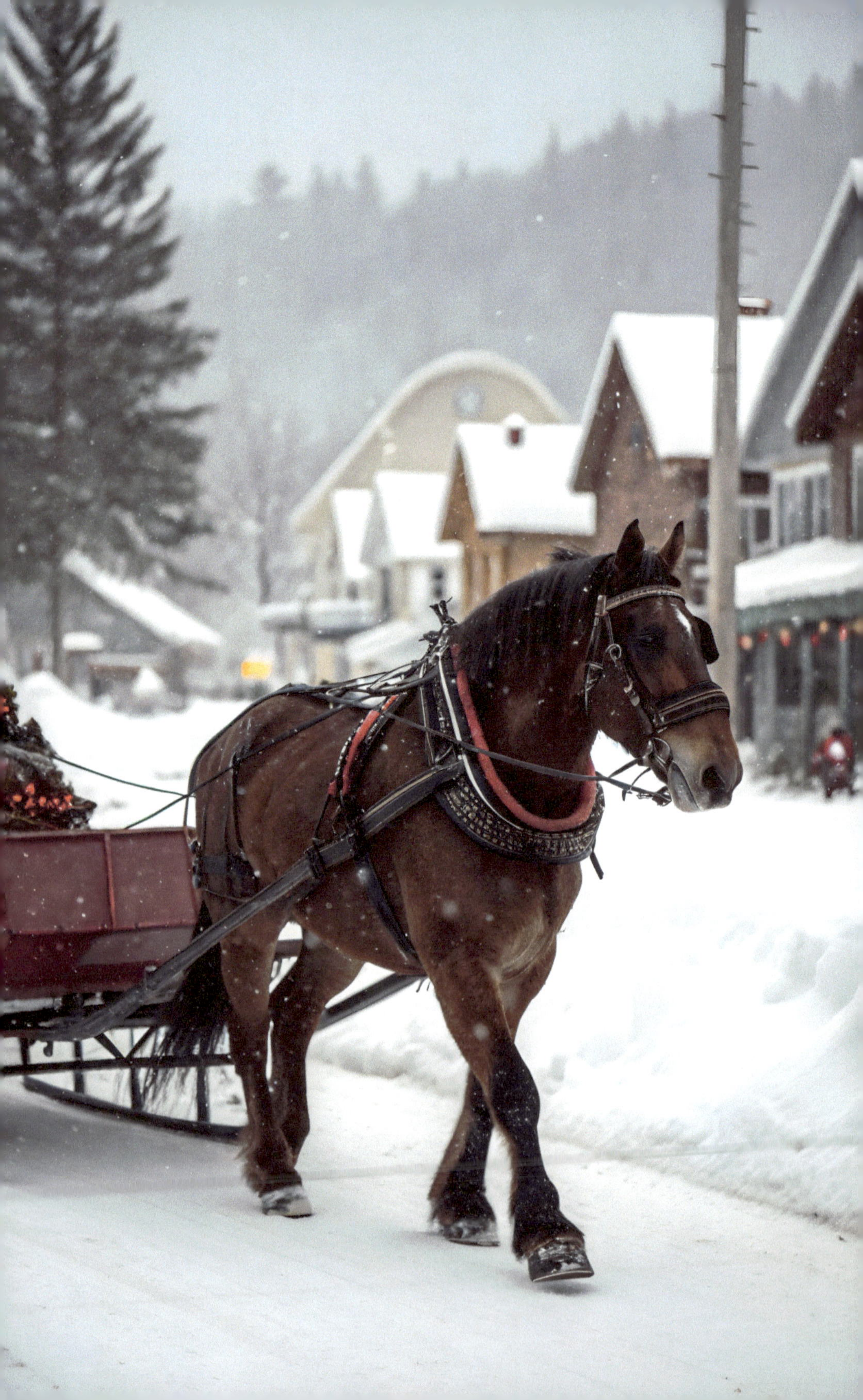

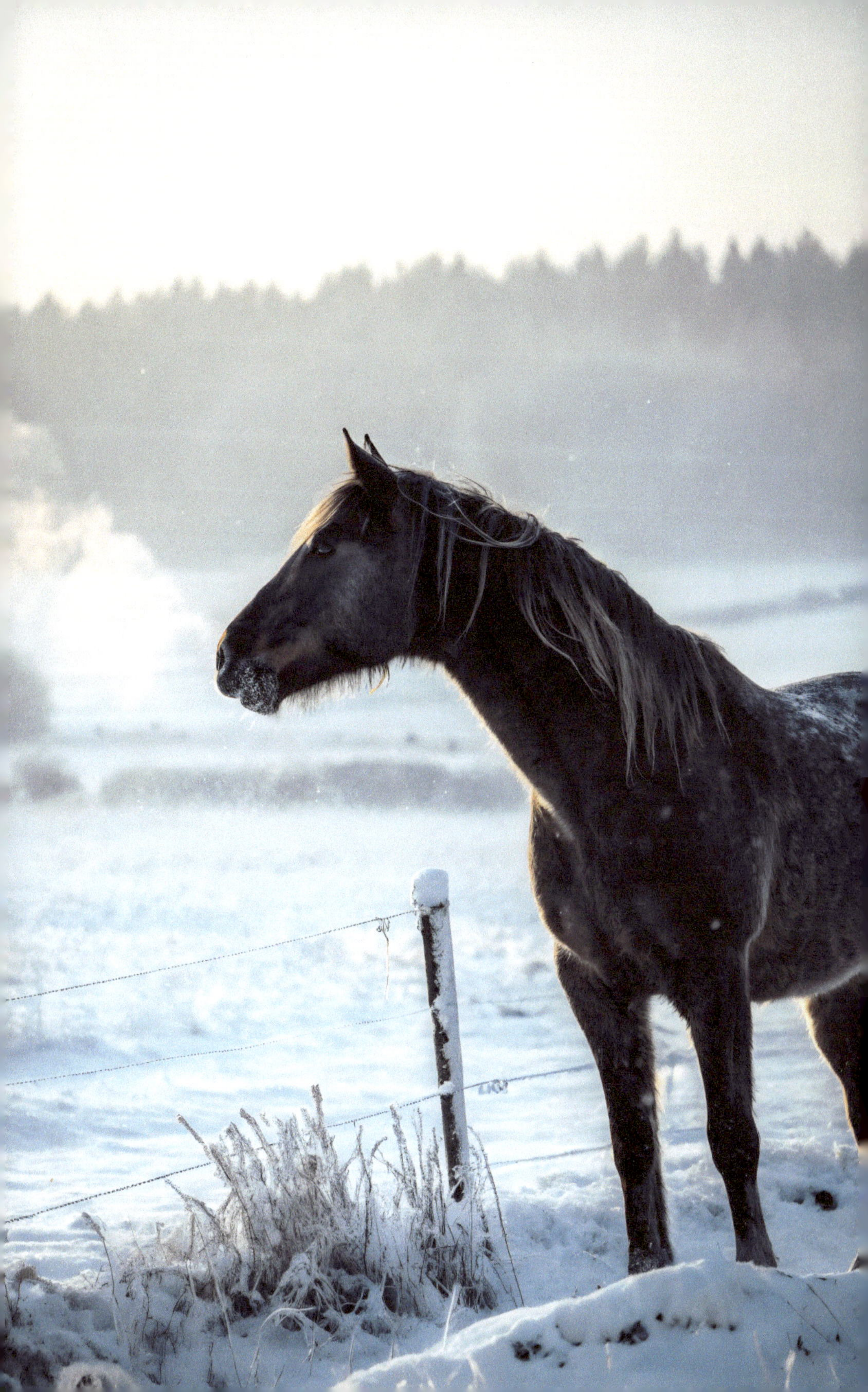

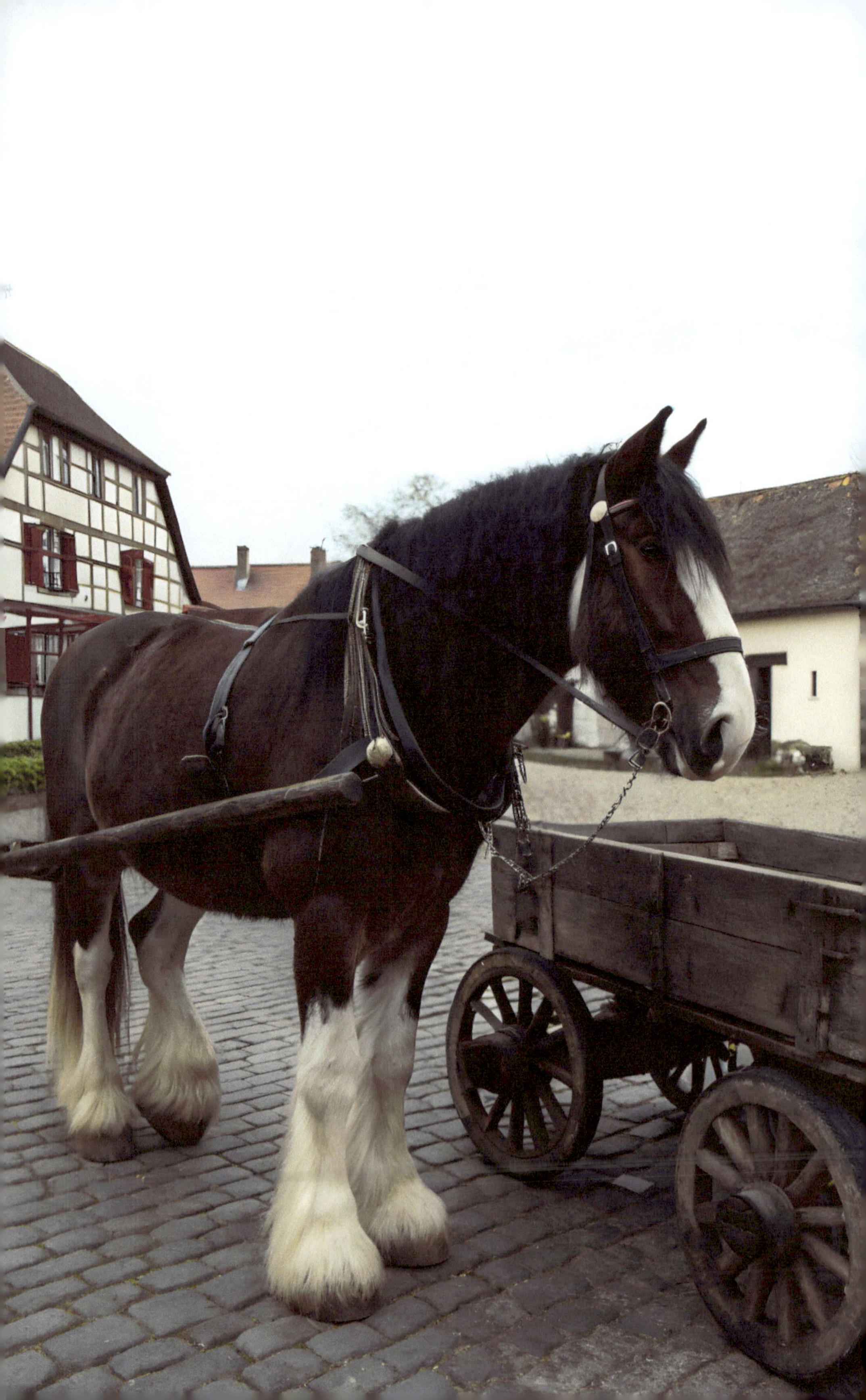

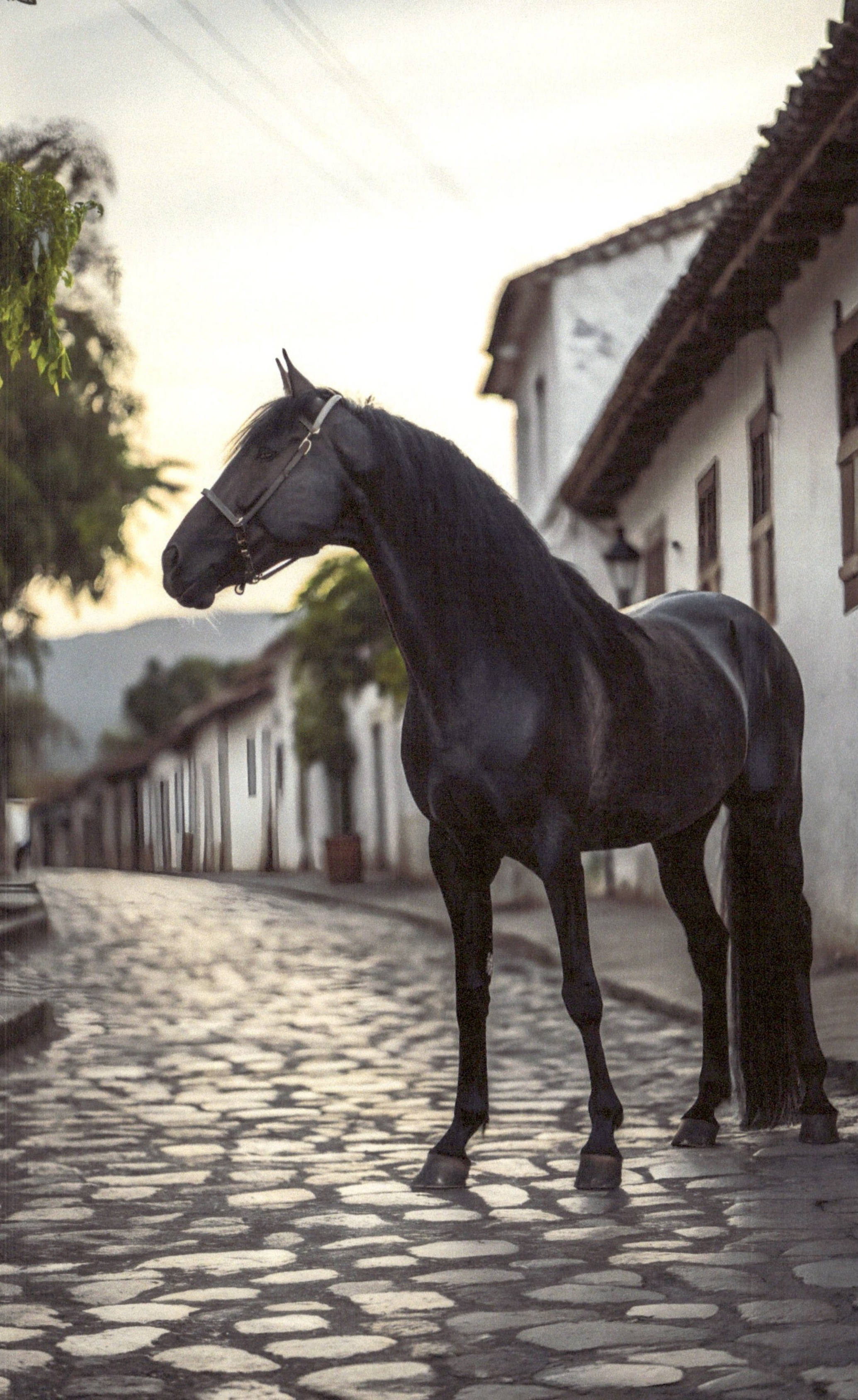

www.ingramcontent.com/pod-product-compliance
Lightning Source LLC
Chambersburg PA
CBHW040244240726
48664CB00001B/252